The Best of Mr. Food®

"Join me in the kitchen with this new cookbook chock-full of my favorite easy recipes! 'OOH IT'S SO GOOD!!®'*"*

Sausage-Rice Dressing, page 112

Stroganoff Casserole,
page 71

Mocha Brownie Cake,
page 157

The Best of Mr. Food®

Oxmoor
House®

Library of Congress Control Number: 00-131676
ISBN: 0-8487-2375-9

Printed in the United States of America
Fifth Printing 2002

Mr. Food®, the Caricature Logo, and OOH IT'S SO GOOD!! are registered marks owned by Ginsburg Enterprises Incorporated.

Ginsburg Enterprises Incorporated
    Vice President, Publishing: Caryl Ginsburg Fantel
    Vice President, Creative Business Development: Howard Rosenthal

Oxmoor House, Inc.
    Editor-in-Chief: Nancy Fitzpatrick Wyatt
    Senior Foods Editor: Susan Carlisle Payne
    Senior Editor, Copy and Homes: Olivia Kindig Wells
    Art Director: James Boone

THE BEST OF MR. FOOD®
    Editor: Keri Bradford Anderson
    Copy Editor: Donna Baldone
    Associate Art Director: Cynthia R. Cooper
    Designer: Kelly Davis
    Editorial Assistant: Suzanne Powell
    Publishing Systems Administrator: Rick Tucker
    Director, Test Kitchens: Elizabeth Tyler Luckett
    Assistant Director, Test Kitchens: Julie Christopher
    Recipe Editor: Gayle Hays Sadler
    Test Kitchens Staff: Gretchen Feldtman, Rebecca Mohr, Jan A. Smith
    Senior Photographers: Jim Bathie, Charles Walton IV
    Photographers: Ralph Anderson, Tina Cornett, Brit Huckabay
    Senior Photo Stylist: Kay E. Clarke
    Photo Stylists: Virginia R. Cravens, Mary Lyn H. Jenkins, Leslie Byars Simpson
    Director, Production and Distribution: Phillip Lee
    Associate Production Manager: Theresa L. Beste
    Production Assistant: Faye Porter Bonner

    Contributors:
    Indexer: Mary Ann Laurens
    Test Kitchens: Kathleen Royal Phillips, Kate M. Wheeler, R.D.
    Intern: Jane E. Lorberau

Cover: *Chicken in Wine Sauce, page 54*

Contents

Welcome!!

"Does anyone really want to spend hours in the kitchen trying to figure out complicated recipes? I sure don't!! And that's why I'm so excited about sharing all of these great-tasting, quick-and-easy recipes with you in my new cookbook! Every dish is full of old-fashioned flavor, but I've updated and streamlined the recipes to fit today's busy lifestyles. The ingredients are easy to find, and the numbered cooking steps are easy to follow. The results? You can have mouthwatering entrées, breads, sides, and desserts in minutes!! So get set to fix scrumptious dishes that'll have your whole gang saying 'OOH IT'S SO GOOD!!'"

Mr. Food

Party Hearty

"Make your next celebration a smash with these sensational appetizers and beverages. They're ooh-so-easy!**"**

Sweet-and-Spicy Pecans

2 cups

2   cups pecan halves*
2   tablespoons butter, melted

1   tablespoon sugar
1   teaspoon ground cumin
1   teaspoon chili powder
½   teaspoon dried crushed red pepper
¼   teaspoon salt

*Substitute 2 cups whole almonds, skins on, for pecans, if desired.

1 Preheat the oven to 325°. Toss pecans in butter.

2 Combine sugar and remaining 4 ingredients. Sprinkle over pecans, and toss.

3 Spread pecans on an ungreased baking sheet; bake at 325° for 12 to 15 minutes, stirring every 5 minutes. Cool. Store in an airtight container.

Go Nuts!

Once you start poppin' these in your mouth, it's hard to stop snacking! Make 'em ahead for a party or to give as gifts—trust me, people will want this recipe! My buttery coating goes well with any nuts—especially whole ones. Best of all, you can keep these nuts up to a week if you seal them in an airtight container.

Orange-Sour Cream Dip

2½ cups

1   (6-ounce) can frozen orange juice
        concentrate, thawed and undiluted
1   (3.4-ounce) package vanilla instant
        pudding mix
1¼ cups milk

¼   cup sour cream
Assorted fresh fruit

1 Combine first 3 ingredients in a
medium bowl, stirring with a wire
whisk until mixture is blended.

2 Stir in sour cream. Cover and chill at
least 2 hours. Serve with fresh fruit.

❝I'm always looking for delicious recipes I can just throw together in minutes, and this one tops my list! I make this tangy dip extra creamy by using vanilla pudding as its base.❞

Chunky Guacamole

2¾ cups

2 small avocados, peeled and cubed (about 1½ cups)
2 tablespoons lemon juice
1 large clove garlic, halved

1 medium onion, chopped (¾ cup)
1 (4.5-ounce) can chopped green chiles, drained
½ teaspoon salt
¼ teaspoon pepper
½ teaspoon hot sauce

1 medium tomato, seeded and chopped (about 1 cup)
4 green onions, chopped
Tortilla chips

1 Position knife blade in food processor bowl; add avocado, lemon juice, and garlic. Process 20 seconds, stopping once to scrape down sides.

2 Add onion and next 4 ingredients; pulse 10 times or until mixture is chunky.

3 Transfer mixture to a medium bowl; stir in tomato and green onions. Serve with tortilla chips.

66 Avocados are high in fat, and they account for all the fat in my guacamole. But you can cut the fat by half and keep the creamy texture when you substitute a 15-ounce can of garbanzo beans, rinsed and drained, for one of the avocados. Simply add the beans to the food processor at the same time you add an avocado. 99

Tortilla Roll-ups

50 roll-ups

2   (8-ounce) packages cream cheese
2   green onions, finely chopped
1   (1-ounce) envelope Ranch-style
        dressing mix
5   (10") flour tortillas

¾   cup finely chopped pimiento-stuffed
        olives
¾   cup finely chopped ripe olives
1   (4.5-ounce) can chopped green
        chiles, drained
1   (4-ounce) jar diced pimiento,
        drained

1 Combine first 3 ingredients; stir well. Spread evenly over 1 side of each tortilla.

2 Combine olives and remaining 3 ingredients; spread over cream cheese layer. Roll up tortillas tightly, jellyroll fashion. Wrap in plastic wrap, and chill at least 2 hours or up to 2 days.

3 To serve, remove plastic wrap, and cut each roll into 1"-thick slices.

Here's a Meaty Variation

Deli-Style Roll-ups: Substitute 3 tablespoons spicy brown mustard for dressing mix in cream cheese mixture. Substitute 2 (2½-ounce) packages thinly sliced ham, turkey, or roast beef and 5 large lettuce leaves for olives, green chiles, and pimientos. Place lettuce over cream cheese layer. Top each with 4 ham slices, if desired. Roll up tightly, and chill as directed. Proceed with Step 3.

Spicy Cranberry Cheese

(pictured on back cover)
10 servings

½ cup whole-berry cranberry sauce
½ cup jalapeño pepper jelly

1 (8-ounce) package cream cheese
Assorted crackers, shortbread cookies

1 Combine cranberry sauce and pepper jelly; stir well.

2 Place cream cheese on a serving plate. Spoon cranberry mixture over cream cheese. Serve with crackers or shortbread cookies.

"For a fancy gathering, you can shape the cream cheese in a small salad mold. You'll probably need to double the ingredients to have enough cream cheese to mold. Just soften the cream cheese, and beat it at medium speed of an electric beater until creamy; spread it in a 2-cup mold lined with plastic wrap. Cover and chill it at least 8 hours. Unmold it, remove the plastic, and top the cheese with the cranberry mixture."

Italian Cheese Stack

12 appetizer servings

1   pound thinly sliced provolone cheese

1   (3.5-ounce) jar pesto sauce

¾   pound thinly sliced salami

¼   cup Italian salad dressing

Baguette slices, breadsticks, crackers

1 Place 1 slice of cheese on a large piece of heavy-duty plastic wrap; spread 1 teaspoon pesto over cheese. Top evenly with 3 slices salami, over-lapping slices. Brush salami lightly with salad dressing. Repeat layers, using all of cheese, pesto, salami, and salad dressing, and ending with cheese.

2 Fold plastic wrap over layers, sealing securely. Place a heavy object, such as a small cast-iron skillet, on top to compress layers. Cover and chill at least 24 hours or up to 3 days.

3 Remove plastic wrap to serve. Cut cheese stack into wedges, using an electric knife or a sharp knife. Serve with baguette slices, breadsticks, or crackers.

Sliced Just Right

For the best results, have your deli thinly slice the provolone cheese and salami for this appetizer. Packaged, pre-sliced cheeses and salami are too thick for this recipe.

Hot Seafood Dip

9 cups

2 cups mayonnaise
1 cup freshly grated Parmesan cheese
5 green onions, chopped
3 jalapeño peppers, seeded and
   chopped
2 tablespoons lemon juice
2 or 3 drops of hot sauce

1 pound steamed and peeled small
   shrimp (see box below)
1 pound fresh lump crabmeat, drained
2 (14-ounce) cans artichoke hearts,
   drained and finely chopped
½ teaspoon salt

⅓ cup sliced almonds

Melba toast rounds

1 Preheat the oven to 375°. Combine first 6 ingredients in a large bowl; stir well.

2 Add shrimp, crabmeat, artichoke hearts, and salt; stir well.

3 Spoon mixture into a greased 2-quart baking dish. Sprinkle with almonds.

4 Bake at 375° for 25 minutes or until mixture is thoroughly heated. Serve with melba toast rounds.

"When I entertain, time's important! In this recipe, I use fresh shrimp already steamed and peeled. You can get 'em at your supermarket—just call ahead or visit the seafood department first. That way the shrimp will be ready when you finish shopping! If you want to steam and peel your own shrimp, you'll need to buy 2 pounds unpeeled shrimp. If small shrimp aren't available, just buy medium-size shrimp and cut 'em in half!"

Steak Strips Olé

3 dozen

36 (6") wooden skewers
1 (1- to 1½-pound) flank steak

⅓ cup lime juice
2 tablespoons vegetable oil
1 tablespoon water
2 teaspoons chili powder
1 teaspoon ground cumin
2 cloves garlic, minced
½ teaspoon salt

Garnish: lime rind curls

1 Soak wooden skewers in water 30 minutes. Cut steak diagonally across grain into ¼"-thick strips. Thread beef evenly onto skewers, weaving back and forth; place in a shallow dish.

2 Combine lime juice and next 6 ingredients in a bowl; pour over beef. Cover and chill 30 minutes.

3 Preheat the grill. Cook beef, without grill lid, over medium coals (300° to 350°) 3 minutes on each side or to desired degree of doneness. Garnish, if desired.

Dining in Tonight?

Thin strips of flank steak spiked with Southwestern seasonings are sure to be a hit, so make a meal of this no-fuss appetizer. Serve it on skewers or wrap the meat in warmed tortillas with shredded cheese, lettuce, tomato, or any of your favorite Tex-Mex toppings. It'll serve six as a main dish. Bet it will be a hit with everyone in your family!

Cheesy Chicken Pita Wedges

64 appetizers

12 ounces cream cheese, softened
2 cups diced cooked chicken
1½ cups (6 ounces) shredded Monterey
    Jack cheese with peppers
3 green onions, chopped
¼ cup chopped purple onion
¼ cup sour cream
2 cloves garlic, minced
1 teaspoon ground cumin
1 teaspoon chili powder
¼ teaspoon salt
1 cup chopped red bell pepper
    (optional)

4 (6") pita bread rounds

Garnishes: sliced green onions,
        shredded Monterey Jack cheese
        with peppers, salsa

1 Preheat the oven to 375°. Combine first 10 ingredients and, if desired, red bell pepper in a large bowl; stir well.

2 Slice each pita horizontally to make 2 rounds. Spread chicken mixture evenly over rough sides of pita rounds. Using a pizza cutter, slice each round into 8 wedges; place wedges on ungreased baking sheets.

3 Bake at 375° for 8 to 10 minutes or until topping is golden and bubbly. Garnish, if desired. Serve immediately.

Thai Wings

8 servings

24   chicken wings (about 4½ pounds)

½   cup frozen pineapple-orange-apple juice concentrate, thawed and undiluted
⅓   cup soy sauce
2   tablespoons creamy peanut butter
2   tablespoons minced fresh cilantro
1   tablespoon minced fresh ginger
1   clove garlic, pressed
1   teaspoon sugar

1 Place chicken wings in a heavy-duty, zip-top plastic bag.

2 Stir together juice concentrate and remaining 6 ingredients. Pour mixture over wings; seal bag, and chill 8 hours, turning occasionally.

3 Preheat the oven to 375°. Remove wings from marinade, discarding marinade. Place wings on a rack in a shallow roasting pan.

4 Bake at 375° for 30 to 35 minutes or until chicken is done.

Just Wing It!

To turn these wings into a crowd-pleasin' appetizer, cut off the wing tips and discard, if desired; cut the wings in half at the joint, and proceed with Step 1. For variety, you can make this recipe with 3 pounds of pork back ribs. To serve both the wings and the pork, just double the marinade; then proceed with Step 1.

Mini Hot Turkey Sandwiches

6 dozen

3   (8-ounce) packages small party rolls on aluminum trays

1   (3-ounce) package cream cheese, softened
½   cup mayonnaise
½   teaspoon curry powder
⅛   teaspoon ground red pepper
2   tablespoons chutney

¾   pound very thinly sliced smoked turkey
1   (16-ounce) can whole-berry cranberry sauce
¼   cup minced onion

1 Preheat the oven to 350°. Remove rolls from aluminum trays. Slice rolls in half horizontally, using a serrated knife. Return bottom halves of rolls to trays.

2 Combine cream cheese and next 3 ingredients. Beat at low speed of an electric beater until smooth. Stir in chutney. Spread cream cheese mixture evenly on cut sides of top halves of rolls.

3 Place turkey on bottom halves of rolls. Combine cranberry sauce and onion; stir well. Spread cranberry mixture over turkey. Cover with tops of rolls.

4 Cover and bake at 350° for 20 to 30 minutes or until sandwiches are thoroughly heated. To serve, cut sandwiches apart with a sharp knife.

Prepare to Party!

The beauty of these party sandwiches is that you can make a batch to eat right away and then freeze the rest without baking. Or you can make them for a party a month early! Simply wrap them in foil, and freeze. When you're ready for 'em, bake the sandwiches, still frozen and wrapped in foil, at 350° for 50 minutes or until thoroughly heated.

Pepperoni Pinwheels

12 servings

1   (10-ounce) can refrigerated pizza crust

1   cup (4 ounces) shredded mozzarella cheese

½   cup grated Parmesan cheese

1   (3.5-ounce) package sliced pepperoni, chopped

½   cup spaghetti sauce or pizza sauce, heated

1 Preheat the oven to 400°. Unroll pizza crust on a cutting board; roll crust into a 9" x 12" rectangle. Sprinkle with cheeses and pepperoni.

2 Roll up, starting at long side; moisten edge with water, and pinch seam to seal. Cut into 1"-wide slices. Place slices 1" apart, cut side down, on a lightly greased 10" x 15" jellyroll pan; flatten slices slightly.

3 Bake at 400° for 12 to 14 minutes or until golden. Serve immediately with warm spaghetti sauce.

❝ I've wrapped up pepperoni and Parmesan cheese in convenient refrigerated pizza crust for appetizers that won't be around for long! Spaghetti sauce or pizza sauce makes a quick dippin' sauce for 'em. ❞

Crispy Wontons

40 wontons

1   (7-ounce) can tiny shrimp, drained
½   pound ground pork
3   tablespoons chopped water
      chestnuts
2   green onions, chopped
1   large egg
2   tablespoons chopped fresh cilantro
1   teaspoon minced garlic
½   teaspoon salt

1   (16-ounce) package wonton
      wrappers

3   cups vegetable oil

1 Position knife blade in food processor bowl; add first 8 ingredients. Pulse 8 times or until blended.

2 Spoon 1 rounded teaspoonful of pork mixture onto center of each wonton wrapper; moisten edges with water. Fold wonton in half to form a triangle, pressing edges together to seal. Reserve any remaining wonton wrappers for another use.

3 Pour oil into a large Dutch oven; heat to 350°. Fry wontons, in batches, 2 minutes or until golden, turning once. Drain wontons on paper towels. Serve with hot mustard and sweet-and-sour sauce.

Bacon-Wrapped Shrimp Bites

40 appetizers

40   unpeeled large fresh shrimp

20   bacon slices
2½ cups barbecue sauce, divided

1 Peel shrimp, and devein, if desired. Set shrimp aside.

2 Preheat the oven to Broil. Cut bacon slices in half crosswise. Wrap bacon pieces around shrimp, securing with wooden toothpicks; place on a lightly greased rack in a broiler pan. Pour ½ cup barbecue sauce into a small bowl (set aside remaining 2 cups sauce to serve with cooked shrimp). Brush shrimp with ½ cup barbecue sauce in bowl.

3 Broil shrimp 3 inches from heat (with electric oven door partially opened) 2½ minutes on each side or until bacon is crisp.

4 Heat reserved 2 cups barbecue sauce, and serve with shrimp.

Quick Fixes

These easy appetizers are sure to be a hit at your next gathering! With just three ingredients, you can quickly make 'em ahead. Then all you'll have to do is pop 'em in the oven right before guests arrive. Heat extra barbecue sauce and serve it as a dipping sauce!

Candy Apple Cider

16 cups

1   gallon apple cider
1   (9-ounce) bag red cinnamon candies
       (about 1 cup)
1   orange, thinly sliced
2   tablespoons frozen lemonade
       concentrate

1 Combine all ingredients in a large Dutch oven. Bring mixture to a boil; reduce heat, and simmer, uncovered, 30 minutes, stirring occasionally. Serve cider hot.

" I like to have a pot of this cider simmering when guests arrive—it gives the house a real welcoming aroma. The cinnamon candies in this punch remind me of a candy apple! Shhh . . . they're my secret ingredient!"

Old-Fashioned Chocolate Milk Shakes

2 cups

2   cups chocolate ice cream
½   cup milk
½   teaspoon vanilla extract
2   tablespoons malt-flavored chocolate
     drink mix (optional)

1 Process all ingredients in container of an electric blender until smooth, stopping once to scrape down sides. Serve immediately.

Quick Change Artist!
Chocolate-Peanut Butter Milk Shakes: Add 3 tablespoons creamy peanut butter to the ingredients in the electric blender.

Minty Lime Sherbet Punch

6 cups

1	cup water
½	cup sugar
4	fresh mint leaves, coarsely chopped

2	cups limeade (made from concentrate)
1	quart lime sherbet, softened

Garnish: fresh mint sprigs

1 Combine first 3 ingredients in a small saucepan; stir well. Bring to a boil; reduce heat, and simmer, uncovered, 10 minutes. Discard mint leaves. Cover and chill.

2 Combine sugar mixture and limeade in a small punch bowl; stir well. Spoon softened sherbet into limeade mixture, and stir until partially melted. Serve immediately. Garnish, if desired.

" This punch has a delicate mint flavor, but if you're a fan of fresh mint, toss a few more leaves into the sugar mixture. In this recipe, I like to experiment with the different varieties of mint from my garden. Different kinds give subtle but fun flavor surprises! "

Margarita Punch

24 cups

2 (12-ounce) cans frozen limeade concentrate, undiluted
1 (12-ounce) can frozen lemonade concentrate, undiluted
1 (1-ounce) bottle orange extract
6 cups water

1 (3-liter) bottle lemon-lime carbonated beverage, chilled
Garnish: lime slices

1 Stir together first 4 ingredients in a punch bowl or pitcher.

2 Stir in carbonated beverage just before serving, and pour over crushed ice; serve immediately. Garnish, if desired.

Make Mine a "Mocktail."
Cocktail margaritas are traditionally served in a glass that's rimmed with salt. You can jazz up this nonalcoholic beverage for a knockout "mocktail." For authenticity, rub the rim of each glass with a lime wedge; dip the rim in a plate of coarse salt, and turn the rim of the glass so that salt sticks to it. Or, even quicker, give the rims a quick "dip" in the punch and then spin them in the salt.

Cold Buttered Rum Drink

3 ½ cups

1   quart butter pecan ice cream
½   cup dark rum

1 Process both ingredients in container of an electric blender until smooth, stopping once to scrape down sides. Pour into glasses; serve immediately.

A Frosty Treat in a Flash!
Nothing could be quicker and easier than this ice cream-rum beverage. Just toss the two ingredients in the blender, give it a swirl, and you've got a simply sensational drink!

Orange Fizz

4 cups

1½ cups orange juice
2   cups orange sherbet
1   cup vodka or gin
Garnish: fresh orange slices

1 Process first 3 ingredients in an electric blender until smooth, stopping once to scrape down sides. Pour into stemmed glasses. Garnish, if desired.

" A generous dose of vodka or gin gives this citrus refresher a mighty punch. When kids are going to be at the party, I create a child-friendly version by replacing the alcohol with sparkling water. "

Cranberry Mulled Wine

3½ cups

2   cups cranberry juice cocktail
½   cup firmly packed brown sugar
3   whole cloves
3   whole allspice

1½ cups dry red wine
Garnish: cinnamon sticks

1 Combine first 4 ingredients in a saucepan; bring to a boil over medium heat, stirring until sugar dissolves.

2 Reduce heat; simmer, uncovered, 5 minutes. Remove from heat. Discard whole spices. Stir in wine. Serve warm, and garnish, if desired.

A Simmering Favorite for All Ages!
Some versions of mulled wine simmer for a long time to develop the taste. My variation is speedy and still has plenty of flavor that everyone will love. If youngsters are around, make them a batch of this toasty beverage without the wine.

Fancy Schmancy Dinners

66Fancy doesn't have to mean spending hours in the kitchen! Just fix these fast entrées for fantastic meals in a flash!99

Pepper and Garlic Flounder

6 servings

6   (4-ounce) flounder fillets
¼   cup soy sauce
2   tablespoons minced garlic
1½ tablespoons lemon juice
2   teaspoons sugar

1   tablespoon mixed peppercorns,
     crushed

1 Place fillets in a shallow baking dish. Combine soy sauce and next 3 ingredients; pour over fillets. Cover and marinate in refrigerator 30 minutes.

2 Preheat the oven to Broil. Remove fillets from marinade; discard marinade. Sprinkle fillets evenly with peppercorns, pressing firmly so that pepper adheres to fillets.

3 Place fillets on a rack of broiler pan coated with nonstick cooking spray. Broil 5½ inches from heat (with electric oven door partially opened) 8 to 10 minutes or until fish flakes easily when tested with a fork.

> ### Take a Bow!
> You'll net a lot of applause with this flavorful fish dinner—a four-ingredient marinade and some peppercorns are all it takes for a simple entrée.

Grouper à la Mango

4 servings

1½ cups finely chopped fresh mango
     (about 2 mangoes)
½ cup finely chopped red bell pepper
⅓ cup finely chopped purple onion
¼ cup chopped fresh cilantro
2 tablespoons fresh lime juice
¼ teaspoon salt

4 (4-ounce) grouper fillets
¼ teaspoon ground red pepper
¼ teaspoon salt

1 Preheat the oven to 425°. Combine first 6 ingredients in a small bowl; toss well. Set mango salsa aside, or chill, if desired.

2 Sprinkle fillets evenly with ground red pepper and ¼ teaspoon salt; arrange in a lightly greased 7" x 11" baking dish.

3 Bake at 425° for 20 minutes or until fish flakes easily when tested with a fork. Serve with mango salsa.

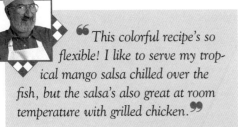

This colorful recipe's so flexible! I like to serve my tropical mango salsa chilled over the fish, but the salsa's also great at room temperature with grilled chicken.

Crab-Stuffed Orange Roughy

8 servings

1   pound fresh lump crabmeat

1   large egg, lightly beaten
⅔   cup fine, dry breadcrumbs
       (store-bought)
1   tablespoon finely chopped onion
1   tablespoon finely chopped red or
       green bell pepper
1   tablespoon chopped fresh parsley
1   tablespoon mayonnaise
2   teaspoons seafood seasoning
1½ teaspoons dry mustard
1   teaspoon hot pepper sauce

8   (8-ounce) orange roughy fillets
¼   cup butter, melted
2   tablespoons lemon juice
½   teaspoon paprika

1 Drain crabmeat, and remove any bits of shell.

2 Preheat the oven to 350°. Combine egg and next 8 ingredients in a large bowl; add crabmeat, stirring gently.

3 Spoon ½ cup crabmeat mixture on each fillet. Starting at a short end, roll up fillets; place, seam side down, in a lightly greased 9" x 13" baking dish. Combine butter and lemon juice; drizzle over fillets. Sprinkle with paprika.

4 Bake, uncovered, at 350° for 30 minutes or until fish flakes easily when tested with a fork.

Blackened Snapper

4 servings

3 tablespoons paprika
1 tablespoon lemon pepper
2½ teaspoons garlic powder
2½ teaspoons dried basil, crushed
1½ teaspoons onion powder
1½ teaspoons ground red pepper
1½ teaspoons dried thyme
½ teaspoon salt

4 red snapper fillets (about 1½ pounds)
½ cup butter, melted

Lemon wedges

1 Combine first 8 ingredients in a large shallow dish.

2 Dip fillets in butter, and dredge in spice mixture.

3 Heat a large cast-iron skillet or heavy aluminum skillet over medium-high heat 10 minutes or until very hot.

4 Cook fillets, 2 at a time, 2 to 3 minutes on each side or until fish flakes easily when tested with a fork. Serve with lemon wedges.

Blackening Basics

You won't need to grease your pan for this recipe because the fish cooks quickly on the high heat. But make sure you've preheated the pan well enough. Otherwise, the fish won't stick to the pan, and you may not get the charring or blackening that gives the fish its great flavor!

Scallops with Tomato-Butter Sauce

(pictured on facing page)

4 servings

2 tablespoons chopped fresh thyme
1 tablespoon chopped fresh rosemary
½ teaspoon salt
¼ teaspoon ground black pepper
⅛ teaspoon dried crushed red pepper
2 cloves garlic, minced
2 tablespoons olive oil
2 tablespoons lemon juice
1½ pounds sea scallops

½ cup fresh orange juice
¼ cup butter, softened
¾ cup seeded and diced tomato
2 tablespoons chopped fresh parsley
Salt and pepper to taste

Garnish: fresh rosemary sprigs

1 Combine first 8 ingredients in a medium bowl. Add scallops, and toss well. Cover and marinate in refrigerator 1 hour.

2 Bring orange juice to a boil in a medium saucepan. Reduce heat, and simmer, uncovered, 10 minutes or until reduced by half. Gently stir in butter, tomato, and parsley. Cook until thoroughly heated, stirring often; add salt and pepper to taste. Set aside, and keep warm.

3 Preheat the grill. Remove scallops from marinade, discarding marinade; thread scallops onto 4 (12") skewers. Coat grill rack with nonstick cooking spray, and place over medium-hot coals (350° to 400°); place skewers on rack. Grill, covered, 4 to 5 minutes on each side or until scallops are opaque. Remove from skewers, if desired. Serve with sauce. Garnish, if desired.

Herb Appeal

Fresh herbs pump up the flavor of sea scallops before grilling. Accompany the scallops with bread, pasta, or rice. You can also serve smaller portions of these tangy scallops as appetizers.

Filet Mignon with Horseradish
Gravy, page 47

Italian Turkey Roll, page 60

Shrimp with Feta Cheese

(pictured on facing page)

4 servings

1	pound unpeeled large fresh shrimp

1 Peel shrimp, and devein, if desired; set shrimp aside.

¾	cup chopped green onions
2	tablespoons chopped fresh parsley
2	tablespoons olive oil
1	(14.5-ounce) can Italian-style tomatoes, drained
¼	teaspoon salt
¼	teaspoon pepper
2	cloves garlic, minced

2 Cook green onions and parsley in hot oil in a large skillet over medium heat, stirring constantly, until onion is tender. Stir in tomatoes and next 3 ingredients; bring to a boil. Cover, reduce heat, and simmer 5 minutes.

½	cup clam juice or vegetable broth

3 Preheat the oven to Broil. Add clam juice to vegetable mixture; cook 5 more minutes. Pour mixture into a 7" x 11" baking dish; set aside.

¼	cup butter, melted
¼	cup dry white wine
1½	teaspoons dried oregano
1	(4-ounce) package crumbled feta cheese

4 Cook shrimp in butter in a small skillet over medium heat 3 minutes or until shrimp turn pink. Spoon shrimp over sauce in baking dish; sprinkle with wine, oregano, and cheese. Broil 5½" from heat (with electric oven door partially opened) 5 minutes. Spoon into individual bowls. Serve with crusty French bread.

66 I have a weak spot for feta cheese and tomatoes, and I think I've found the perfect dish to show 'em off! Ladle the shrimp into soup bowls to catch all the flavorful juices that are released as the mixture cooks. Serve it over rice, pasta, or just with bread to enjoy all of the sauce! 99

Cheesy Shrimp Linguine

6 servings

1   (16-ounce) package dried linguine
2   pounds unpeeled large fresh shrimp

1   small green bell pepper, chopped
       (about ½ cup)
¼   cup chopped onion
2   celery ribs, chopped
¾   cup butter, melted
1   teaspoon all-purpose flour

¼   cup chopped fresh parsley
1   (8-ounce) loaf process cheese
      spread, cubed
1   cup half-and-half

Freshly ground black pepper

1 Cook pasta according to package directions; drain and keep warm. Meanwhile, peel shrimp, and devein, if desired; set shrimp aside.

2 Cook green pepper, onion, and celery in butter in a large skillet over medium-high heat 5 minutes or until tender. Add flour, stirring until blended.

3 Stir in shrimp and parsley; cook 6 minutes or until shrimp turn pink, stirring often. Reduce heat to medium; add cheese spread and half-and-half. Cook, stirring constantly, until cheese melts.

4 Combine pasta and shrimp mixture, tossing gently; sprinkle with black pepper, and serve immediately.

Chicken Change-up

Cheesy Chicken Linguine: Substitute 2 cups chopped cooked chicken for fresh shrimp, but don't cook the chicken 6 minutes as directed for the shrimp in Step 3. Instead, immediately reduce the heat, and add the cheese spread and half-and-half. Proceed with Step 3.

Grilled Asian Pesto Shrimp

4 servings

2 pounds unpeeled medium-size
   fresh shrimp

⅓ cup olive oil
1 tablespoon dark sesame oil
3 tablespoons minced garlic
3 tablespoons chopped fresh basil
1 green onion, chopped
2 teaspoons dried crushed red pepper
1 teaspoon salt
½ teaspoon freshly ground black
   pepper

Nonstick cooking spray

❝My homemade pesto sauce really perks up fresh shrimp! For those who like a little heat, go ahead and marinate the shrimp longer to give them more punch. When it's time to thread the shrimp on the skewers, try my little trick to prevent the shrimp from twirling around—just thread them at both the head and the tail.❞

1 Peel shrimp, and devein, if desired; set shrimp aside.

2 Process olive oil and next 7 ingredients in an electric blender until smooth, stopping once to scrape down sides. Place pesto mixture in a large heavy-duty, zip-top plastic bag. Add shrimp; seal bag securely, and shake until shrimp are coated. Marinate shrimp in refrigerator 1 to 3 hours, turning bag occasionally.

3 Preheat the grill. Remove shrimp from marinade, discarding marinade; thread shrimp onto 12 (10") skewers. Coat food rack with nonstick cooking spray, and place on grill over medium-hot coals (350° to 400°). Place skewers on rack, and grill, uncovered, 3 minutes on each side or until done.

Note: You can substitute commercial pesto and 2 teaspoons dried crushed red pepper for the pesto mixture that's made with olive oil, sesame oil, garlic, basil, green onion, red pepper, salt, and black pepper.

Low-Country Seafood Boil

4 servings

3 quarts water
4 (3-ounce) packages dry shrimp-and-crab boil seasoning
1 teaspoon salt

1½ pounds new potatoes
1 (16-ounce) package frozen pearl or boiling onions
8 frozen half-ears whole kernel corn
2 lemons, cut in half

1½ pounds unpeeled large fresh shrimp
Lemon wedges
Zesty Cocktail Sauce

1 Combine first 3 ingredients in a stockpot or large Dutch oven; bring to a boil.

2 Add potatoes, onions, corn, and lemon halves; return to a boil, and cook 15 minutes or until potatoes are tender.

3 Add shrimp to Dutch oven; cover and cook 5 minutes or until shrimp turn pink. Drain mixture; remove and discard seasoning bags and lemon halves. Serve immediately with lemon wedges and Zesty Cocktail Sauce.

Zesty Cocktail Sauce

1 (12-ounce) bottle cocktail sauce
3 tablespoons prepared horseradish
2 tablespoons lemon juice

Stir together all ingredients; cover and chill. Yield: 1¼ cups.

Mussels Steamed in Wine

5 servings

5	dozen fresh mussels
½	cup butter
1	large onion, chopped
2	shallots, chopped
2	cloves garlic, minced
2½	cups finely chopped fresh parsley
½	teaspoon freshly ground pepper
1½	cups dry white wine
¼	cup fresh lemon juice
3	tablespoons butter

1 Remove beards from mussels, and scrub shells with a brush. Discard opened, cracked, or heavy mussels (they're filled with sand). Keep mussels chilled.

2 Melt ½ cup butter in a large Dutch oven over medium heat. Add onion and next 4 ingredients; cook 5 minutes, stirring occasionally. Pour in wine, and bring to a boil. Cook over medium-high heat 15 minutes or until liquid is reduced to about ¾ cup.

3 Add mussels; cover and steam 4 minutes or until mussels open, shaking Dutch oven several times. Remove from heat; transfer mussels to a serving dish with a slotted spoon, discarding any unopened mussels. Set mussels aside, and keep warm.

4 Place Dutch oven over medium-high heat until hot; stir in lemon juice. Remove from heat; whisk in 3 tablespoons butter. Pour over mussels, and serve immediately.

> *"I love how the rich, buttery sauce coats these fresh mussels. In fact, I always serve this recipe with plenty of French bread so I can sop up every drop of the sauce!"*

Eye-of-Round Roast

8 servings

1   (4½-pound) eye-of-round roast

1   (4-ounce) jar Chinese sweet-hot
        mustard
3   tablespoons olive oil
2   cloves garlic, pressed
2   teaspoons soy sauce
1   teaspoon Worcestershire sauce

Roasted Potatoes, uncooked

1 Place roast on an 11" x 18" piece of heavy-duty aluminum foil.

2 Combine mustard and next 4 ingredients; stir well. Spread over roast. Fold foil over roast to seal. Place in a shallow roasting pan coated with nonstick cooking spray. Chill at least 3 hours or overnight.

3 Preheat the oven to 450°. Remove roast from foil; place in roasting pan. Cover and bake at 450° for 30 minutes. Arrange uncooked Roasted Potatoes around roast. Bake, uncovered, 30 minutes or until potatoes are tender and a meat thermometer inserted in roast registers 145° (medium-rare). Cover and let stand 15 minutes; slice roast.

Roasted Potatoes

4 medium baking potatoes, each cut into
        8 wedges
2 tablespoons olive oil
2 cloves garlic, pressed
1 teaspoon salt
½ teaspoon pepper

Combine all ingredients in a bowl; toss. Bake as directed above in Step 3 above. Yield: 8 servings.

Filet Mignon with Horseradish Gravy

(pictured on page 38)

4 servings

1   (¾-ounce) package brown
      gravy mix
2   tablespoons prepared horseradish

4   (5-ounce) beef tenderloin steaks
¼   teaspoon salt
¼   teaspoon pepper

2   tablespoons butter
1   (8-ounce) package sliced fresh
      mushrooms

1 Preheat the oven to 350°. Prepare gravy according to package directions; stir in horseradish. Set aside.

2 Coat a large nonstick skillet with nonstick cooking spray. Place skillet over medium-high heat until hot; add steaks, and cook 1 minute on each side. (Steaks will be rare.) Place in a lightly greased 1-quart baking dish; sprinkle with salt and pepper.

3 Melt butter in skillet over medium heat. Add mushrooms, and cook, stirring constantly, 5 minutes or until tender. Remove from heat; stir in gravy. Pour gravy over steaks; bake, uncovered, at 350° for 15 minutes or to desired degree of doneness. Serve with mashed potatoes and steamed asparagus, if desired.

" *Butter, salt, and pepper accent the succulent flavor of this great steak. The accompanying gravy is just as simple—I've merely dressed up a package of gravy with horseradish. It makes this entrée worthy of a five-star rating!* "

Oven Beef Burgundy

6 servings

3   tablespoons all-purpose flour
2   tablespoons soy sauce
2   pounds boneless chuck roast, cut
       into 1" pieces

1   (16-ounce) bag baby carrots*
2   large onions, sliced
1   clove garlic, minced
1   cup thinly sliced celery
1   cup dry red wine or beef broth
¼   teaspoon dried marjoram
¼   teaspoon dried thyme
¼   teaspoon salt
¼   teaspoon pepper

1   cup sliced fresh mushrooms

*You can substitute 1 pound carrots, peeled and cut into 1" pieces, for the baby carrots.

1 Preheat the oven to 325°. Combine flour and soy sauce in a 3-quart baking dish. Add beef; toss to coat.

2 Add carrots and next 8 ingredients. Cover and bake at 325° for 1 hour.

3 Add mushrooms; cover and bake 2 more hours. Serve over rice, noodles, or toast points.

Let Your Oven Do the Work!

Don't let this recipe make you feel guilty—guilty that you didn't slave for hours in the kitchen!! Just throw everything in the dish, stick it in the oven, and forget about it until it's time to add the mushrooms!

Cheese-Stuffed Veal Marsala

4 servings

4   (4- to 6-ounce) lean boneless veal
     chops (1" thick)

½   cup grated Romano cheese
2   tablespoons minced fresh oregano
     or 2 teaspoons dried oregano

¼   cup all-purpose flour
¼   teaspoon salt
½   teaspoon freshly ground pepper

1   tablespoon olive oil
½   cup canned beef broth
¼   cup dry Marsala or other dry
     red wine

1 Cut chops in half horizontally to within ½" of 1 long edge. Open chops, and place between two sheets of heavy-duty plastic wrap; flatten to ¼" thickness, using a meat mallet or rolling pin.

2 Combine cheese and oregano, tossing lightly; place one-fourth of mixture on 1 cut half of each veal chop. Fold chops to enclose filling; press edges of chops together, and secure with wooden toothpicks.

3 Combine flour, salt, and pepper in a shallow dish; coat chops on all sides with mixture.

4 Pour oil into a large nonstick skillet; place over medium-high heat until hot. Add chops to skillet; cook 3 minutes on each side or until browned. Add broth and wine; bring to a boil. Reduce heat, and simmer, uncovered, 15 minutes, turning chops occasionally.

5 To serve, remove toothpicks from chops. Place chops on individual serving plates, and spoon pan juices over chops.

Quick Lamb Bourguignon

3 servings

1 pound lean boneless leg of lamb

2 tablespoons olive oil

1 cup frozen pearl onions, thawed
2 cloves garlic, minced

1 cup canned beef broth
½ cup dry red wine
¼ cup strongly brewed coffee
  (at room temperature)
1½ tablespoons all-purpose flour
1 tablespoon tomato paste
¼ teaspoon salt
½ teaspoon pepper

1 Trim fat from lamb. Place lamb between two sheets of heavy-duty plastic wrap, and flatten to ½" thickness, using a meat mallet or rolling pin; cut into 1" pieces.

2 Cook lamb in hot olive oil in a large skillet over medium-high heat 6 minutes or until browned on all sides. Remove meat from skillet; set aside.

3 Add onions to skillet; cook 2 minutes or until lightly browned and tender, stirring often. Add garlic, and cook 30 seconds, stirring often. Remove onion mixture from skillet, and set aside.

4 Pour beef broth and wine into skillet; bring to a boil. Reduce heat, and simmer, uncovered, 5 minutes. Combine coffee and remaining 4 ingredients, stirring until smooth; pour into skillet. Cook, stirring constantly, until sauce is thickened. Add lamb and onion mixture; simmer 10 minutes, stirring occasionally.

Peppercorn Pork Roast

8 servings

1   (2½-pound) lean boneless pork
     loin roast

¼   cup creamy mustard blend

2   cups soft whole wheat breadcrumbs
     (about 4 slices of bread)

3   tablespoons whole assorted
     peppercorns, crushed

1   tablespoon chopped fresh thyme or
     1 teaspoon dried thyme

¼   teaspoon salt

Creamy Peppercorn Sauce

1 Preheat the oven to 325°. Trim fat from roast. Spread mustard blend over roast.

2 Combine breadcrumbs and next 3 ingredients; press breadcrumb mixture evenly onto roast. Place roast on a rack in a roasting pan coated with cooking spray. Insert a meat thermometer into thickest part of roast, if desired. Bake at 325° for 2 hours or until meat thermometer registers 160° (medium). Let roast stand 10 minutes before slicing. Serve with Creamy Peppercorn Sauce.

Creamy Peppercorn Sauce

¾   cup nonfat buttermilk

⅓   cup sour cream

3   tablespoons grated Parmesan cheese

3   tablespoons mayonnaise

1½ tablespoons lemon juice

1½ teaspoons whole assorted
     peppercorns, crushed

¼   teaspoon salt

Combine all ingredients in a small bowl, stirring well. Yield: 1½ cups.

Fresh Breadcrumbs Fast!

You can make fresh breadcrumbs from leftover rolls or sliced bread. A food processor does a quick job of making crumbs. Don't toast the bread; it should be soft for this recipe.

Sunday Dinner Ham

12 servings

1 (5-pound) canned ham
20 whole cloves (optional)

1 (20-ounce) can sliced pineapple, undrained
½ cup firmly packed brown sugar
1 teaspoon dry mustard
¼ teaspoon ground cloves
1 tablespoon white vinegar

9 maraschino cherries

1 Preheat the oven to 325°. Remove ham from can; place ham in a 9" x 13" baking dish. Using a sharp knife, make 20 (¼"-deep) cuts in top of ham in a diamond pattern. Insert whole cloves into ham in center of diamonds, if desired. Bake, uncovered, 30 minutes.

2 Meanwhile, drain pineapple, reserving 2 tablespoons juice. Combine juice, brown sugar, and next 3 ingredients, stirring well.

3 Remove ham from oven; arrange pineapple slices around sides of ham, using toothpicks. Place 1 cherry in center of each pineapple ring. Spoon brown sugar mixture over ham.

4 Bake, uncovered, 45 more minutes, basting occasionally with pan juices. To serve, slice into individual servings, removing toothpicks and whole cloves.

With this recipe, it's easy to dress up a canned ham in a snap. Just make ¼"-deep cuts in the top in a diamond pattern and insert a whole clove into the center of each diamond.

Roasted Chicken with Vegetables

6 servings

⅓ cup olive oil
¼ cup lemon juice
½ teaspoon dried oregano
1 teaspoon salt
¼ teaspoon pepper

1 (3½- to 4-pound) whole chicken

2 carrots, coarsely chopped
  (about ¾ cup)
2 celery ribs, coarsely chopped
  (about ¾ cup)
1 medium onion, coarsely chopped
1 cup chicken broth

1 Stir together first 5 ingredients in a small bowl.

2 Remove giblets from chicken; reserve giblets for another use. Place chicken in a shallow dish; pour oil mixture over chicken. Cover and chill 8 hours.

3 Remove chicken from marinade, discarding marinade. Fold wings under; tie legs together with string, if desired. Place chicken, breast side up, on a rack in a shallow roasting pan. Arrange carrots, celery, and onion around chicken; add chicken broth to pan.

4 Bake at 425° for 1 hour or until a meat thermometer inserted in meaty party of chicken thigh registers 180°.

Slow Cooker Style

You can cook the chicken in a slow cooker, although it won't brown like it does when oven roasted. Remove the giblets, and reserve for another use. Cut chicken in half, and season with salt and pepper. Place chicken, meaty side up, over vegetable mixture. Cover and cook on HIGH setting 3 hours or until a meat thermometer inserted into meaty part of thigh registers 180°.

Chicken in Wine Sauce

(pictured on cover)

4 servings

1	pound sliced fresh mushrooms
1	(3-pound) broiler-fryer chicken, cut up and skinned

1 Preheat the oven to 350°. Place sliced mushrooms in a lightly greased 9" x 13" baking dish. Arrange chicken over mushrooms.

2	tablespoons cornstarch
¼	cup water
2	tablespoons olive oil
¾	cup rosé wine or white Zinfandel
¼	cup soy sauce
1	clove garlic, pressed
2	tablespoons brown sugar
¼	teaspoon dried oregano
Hot cooked rice	

2 Combine cornstarch and water in a small bowl, stirring until smooth. Stir in olive oil and next 5 ingredients; pour over chicken.

3 Bake, uncovered, at 350° for 1 hour or until chicken is done, basting twice. Serve over rice.

" To clean fresh mushrooms, just wipe them off with a damp paper towel. (Washing mushrooms just waterlogs them.) To simplify things, I like to buy fresh mushrooms already cleaned and sliced—most supermarkets sell them that way in 8-ounce packages. Then all I have to do is add them straight to this dish! It's OOH-SO-EASY!"

Mediterranean Chicken Breasts

4 servings

4   bone-in chicken breast halves
8   cloves garlic, crushed
2   tablespoons olive oil
1   teaspoon salt
1   teaspoon freshly ground pepper
2   teaspoons dried oregano

4   lemons, thinly sliced
16 to 20 kalamata olives, pitted

1   (4-ounce) package crumbled
      feta cheese
Garnishes: lemon slices, fresh
      oregano sprigs

1 Preheat the oven to 350°. Lift skin gently from chicken breasts without detaching it; place 2 crushed garlic cloves under skin of each chicken breast. Replace skin. Rub chicken breasts with olive oil, and sprinkle with salt, pepper, and oregano.

2 Place lemon slices in a 9" x 13" baking dish. Arrange chicken breasts over lemon slices. Sprinkle olives around chicken.

3 Bake, uncovered, at 350° for 45 minutes or until done. Transfer to a serving dish, and sprinkle with feta cheese. Garnish, if desired.

Got a Bone to Pick?

Bone-in chicken breasts have three advantages over the boneless variety: a hefty visual appeal, heightened flavor, and a lower price. Now who'd argue with those?

Grilled Lemon Chicken

6 servings

1	small onion, cut into chunks
½	cup lemon juice
⅓	cup vegetable oil
1	tablespoon Worcestershire sauce
1	teaspoon salt
1	teaspoon pepper
⅛	teaspoon hot sauce
6	skinned and boned chicken breast halves

1 Process first 7 ingredients in an electric blender until smooth, stopping once to scrape down sides. Reserve ¼ cup lemon mixture, and chill.

2 Place chicken in a large heavy-duty, zip-top plastic bag; pour remaining lemon mixture over chicken. Seal bag securely, and chill 2 hours, turning bag occasionally.

3 Preheat the grill. Remove chicken from marinade, discarding marinade. Grill chicken, uncovered, over medium-hot coals (350° to 400°) about 7 minutes on each side or until done, basting chicken often with reserved ¼ cup lemon mixture.

Swiss Chicken

6 servings

6   skinned and boned chicken
     breast halves
⅛   teaspoon garlic powder
⅛   teaspoon pepper
6   (4"-square) slices Swiss cheese

1   (10¾-ounce) can cream of chicken
     soup, undiluted
¼   cup milk
2   cups herb-seasoned stuffing mix
¼   cup butter, melted

1 Preheat the oven to 350°. Place chicken in a greased 9" x 13" baking dish; sprinkle with garlic powder and pepper. Top each breast with a cheese slice; set aside.

2 Combine soup and milk, stirring until smooth; pour over chicken. Sprinkle with stuffing mix, and drizzle with butter.

3 Cover and bake at 350° for 50 minutes or until chicken is done.

Lighten Up!

Slash this recipe's fat by 70 percent and its sodium by 80 percent, and keep all the convenience! All you have to do is substitute a cup of shredded reduced-fat Swiss cheese, reduced-fat cream of chicken soup, fat-free milk, and reduced-sodium stuffing mix for their counterparts.

Cranberry-Cornbread Stuffed Cornish Hens

4 servings

1   (6-ounce) package cornbread
      stuffing mix
½   cup water
½   cup thinly sliced celery

1   (8-ounce) container soft cream
      cheese with chives and onions,
      divided
½   cup fresh or frozen cranberries,
      halved
¼   cup coarsely chopped pecans

4   (1- to 1½-pound) Cornish hens
1   tablespoon vegetable oil

1 Preheat the oven to 350°. Combine seasoning packet from stuffing mix, water, and celery in a large saucepan; bring to a boil. Cover, reduce heat, and simmer 5 minutes.

2 Add ¼ cup cream cheese, stirring until blended. Stir in stuffing mix, cranberries, and pecans. Remove from heat; cover and let stand 5 minutes.

3 If desired, place remaining cream cheese under skin of Cornish hens by loosening skin from hens without totally detaching skin. Lightly spoon stuffing mixture into cavities of hens; close opening with skewers. Place hens, breast side up, in a roasting pan; brush hens with oil.

4 Bake at 350° for 1 hour or until hens are done and a meat thermometer inserted in stuffing registers 165°. Remove skewers; serve immediately.

Herbed Turkey

12 servings

1   (12-pound) turkey

2   tablespoons dried parsley flakes
1   tablespoon dried sage
1½ teaspoons salt
1   teaspoon dried marjoram
1   teaspoon dried thyme
1   teaspoon dried savory
½   teaspoon dried rosemary

1   tablespoon all-purpose flour
1   large oven cooking bag

" I think you'll agree this is the juiciest bird you've ever tasted. I've used a roasting bag to lock in moisture. But its biggest advantage? Minimal cleanup—now that's something to cluck about!"

1 Preheat the oven to 325°. Remove giblets and neck from turkey; reserve for another use. Rinse turkey with cold water; pat dry with paper towels.

2 Process parsley flakes and next 6 ingredients in an electric blender 30 seconds. Sprinkle cavity and outside of turkey with herb mixture. Tie ends of turkey legs to tail with cord. Lift wingtips up and over back, and tuck under turkey.

3 Shake flour in a large oven cooking bag; place in a large roasting pan at least 2" deep. Carefully place turkey in bag; seal. Make 6 (½") slits in top of bag, following package directions. Insert a meat thermometer through bag into meaty part of turkey thigh, making sure thermometer does not touch bone. Bake turkey at 325° for 3 hours or until thermometer registers 180°.

4 Remove turkey from oven; carefully cut a large slit in top of bag, and remove turkey. Let turkey stand 20 minutes before slicing. Serve on a large serving platter.

Italian Turkey Roll

(pictured on page 39)

8 servings

1   (2½- to 3-pound) boneless turkey
        breast

6   very thin slices prosciutto or
        deli ham
6   slices provolone cheese
1   (7-ounce) jar roasted red peppers,
        drained and cut into ¼" strips
8   kalamata olives, pitted and chopped
        (about ¼ cup)

2   tablespoons butter
1   tablespoon vegetable oil
1   cup dry white wine or chicken broth

⅓   cup water
Garnish: fresh oregano sprigs

1 Preheat the oven to 350°. Lay turkey breast flat on wax paper, skin side down. Remove tendons, and trim fat, keeping skin intact. From center, slice horizontally (parallel with skin) through the thickest part of each breast almost to outer edge; flip cut piece and breast fillets over to enlarge breast. Pound breast with a meat mallet or rolling pin to flatten and to form a more even thickness (¾" thick).

2 Layer prosciutto and next 3 ingredients over turkey breast. Beginning with 1 short side, roll up turkey, jellyroll fashion. Tie securely with heavy string at 2" intervals.

3 Heat butter and oil in a large heavy skillet over medium heat. Add turkey roll; brown on all sides. Place turkey roll in a roasting pan; add wine. Bake at 350° for 45 minutes or until a meat thermometer inserted in turkey breast registers 170°, basting occasionally with pan drippings.

4 Remove turkey from pan, reserving drippings. Combine reserved drippings and water in a small saucepan; bring to a boil over medium heat. Cook 10 minutes, stirring occasionally. Remove string from turkey roll; slice roll. Drizzle slices with sauce. Garnish, if desired.

" Looking for a turkey entrée that'll feed company without the time and trouble of cooking a full bird? Try my rolled turkey breast—provolone cheese, thin slices of prosciutto, and ripe olives are wrapped up for a dish that'll deliver the compliments!"

Easy Weeknight Suppers

"Have supper on the table in a snap with these family-pleasin' favorites!"

Italian Fish Fillets

4 servings

4   (6-ounce) orange roughy or
       flounder fillets

1   cup marinara sauce
¾   cup (3 ounces) shredded mozzarella
       cheese
1   teaspoon dried Italian seasoning

1 Preheat the oven to 400°. Place fish fillets in a lightly greased 9" x 13" baking dish.

2 Top fillets with marinara sauce. Sprinkle mozzarella cheese over marinara sauce. Sprinkle with Italian seasoning.

3 Bake, uncovered, at 400° for 15 minutes or until fish flakes easily when tested with a fork.

A Simple Supper Solution!

You can use any mild-flavored fish with this recipe. Make a salad and heat up some rolls while this fish bakes, and you'll have dinner on the table in 20 minutes!

Crunchy Potato Fish Fry

6 servings

1   (2-ounce) envelope instant mashed
      potato granules
2   tablespoons sesame seeds

1   large egg, lightly beaten
1   tablespoon lemon juice
1   teaspoon salt
⅛   teaspoon pepper
1   (24-ounce) package or 2 (12-ounce)
      packages frozen fish fillets, thawed

¼   cup vegetable oil
Lemon wedges (optional)

1 Combine potato granules and sesame seeds in a large shallow dish.

2 Combine egg and next 3 ingredients; stir well. Dip fish in egg mixture, and dredge in potato mixture.

3 Heat 2 tablespoons oil in a large skillet over medium-high heat; fry half of fish in oil 3 minutes on each side or until golden. Drain fish on paper towels. Repeat procedure with remaining oil and fish. Serve fish with lemon wedges, if desired.

"Instant mashed potatoes are the secret to my crunchy coating for fish. Look for frozen fish fillets such as whiting, pollock, ocean perch, or cod in your grocer's freezer section."

No Ordinary Tuna Casserole

4 servings

1   (5-ounce) package egg noodles

1   (10¾-ounce) can cream of
      mushroom soup, undiluted
1   (5-ounce) can evaporated milk
1   (6-ounce) can solid white tuna in
      spring water, drained and flaked
1   (8.5-ounce) can green peas, drained
⅓   cup finely chopped onion
1   cup (4 ounces) shredded Cheddar
      cheese
1½ teaspoons pepper

1   cup tiny fish-shaped cheese crackers

1 Preheat the oven to 350°. Cook egg noodles according to package directions; drain.

2 Stir in soup and next 6 ingredients; spoon into a lightly greased 8" square baking dish.

3 Bake at 350° for 25 minutes. Coarsely crumble half of crackers; sprinkle around edges of casserole. Place remaining whole crackers in the center. Bake 5 more minutes or until casserole is thoroughly heated.

❝ I've pumped up this comfort food casserole by updating the usual cheese topping with those crafty cheesy fish crackers. It's a knockout one-dish dinner! ❞

Oyster Po'boys

4 servings

8 slices bacon

Vegetable oil
1 (7-ounce) package cornmeal mix
¼ teaspoon salt
¼ teaspoon pepper
1 (12-ounce) container fresh Select oysters, drained*
2 large eggs, lightly beaten

1 medium tomato, seeded and chopped
1½ cups rémoulade sauce (store-bought; see box below)
4 (6") French bread rolls, split horizontally and toasted
Lettuce leaves

* Substitute 1 pound medium-size fresh shrimp, peeled, for oysters, if desired.

1 Place bacon on a microwave-safe rack in a 7" x 11" baking dish; cover with paper towels. Microwave at HIGH setting 8 to 10 minutes or until bacon is crisp. Drain.

2 Pour oil to depth of 2" in a Dutch oven; heat to 375°. Combine cornmeal mix, salt, and pepper in a medium bowl. Dip oysters in egg; dredge in cornmeal mixture. Fry oysters, in batches, 1½ to 2 minutes or until golden, turning once. Drain well on paper towels.

3 Combine tomato and rémoulade sauce; spread on cut surfaces of rolls. Arrange lettuce, bacon, and oysters on bottom halves of rolls; cover with tops. Serve immediately.

Note: I prepared the bacon in a 700-watt microwave oven. Cooking times may vary if your wattage is different.

A Saucy Sandwich
This New Orleans classic sandwich gets its big taste from rémoulade sauce—a sharp-flavored French sauce made with mayonnaise, mustard, capers, pickles, and spices. Find it on the condiments aisle in the supermarket.

Luau Beef Kabobs

8 to 10 servings

1 (20-ounce) can pineapple chunks, undrained
½ cup firmly packed brown sugar
⅔ cup cider vinegar
⅔ cup ketchup
¼ cup soy sauce
2 teaspoons ground ginger

3 pounds boneless sirloin tip roast, cut into 1½" cubes

8 to 10 (12") wooden skewers
1 (8-ounce) package fresh mushrooms
2 small purple onions, quartered
1 large red bell pepper, cut into 1" pieces
1 large green bell pepper, cut into 1" pieces
Hot cooked rice

1 Drain pineapple, reserving juice. Combine pineapple juice, sugar, and next 4 ingredients, mixing well.

2 Place beef cubes in a large shallow dish; pour half of marinade over beef. Cover and marinate 2 to 8 hours in refrigerator. Chill remaining marinade and pineapple chunks.

3 Preheat the grill. Soak wooden skewers in water 30 minutes. Drain meat, discarding marinade. Alternate meat, pineapple chunks, mushrooms, onions, and red and green bell peppers on skewers.

4 Place kabobs on grill rack; grill, covered, over medium-hot coals (350° to 400°) 10 to 15 minutes or to desired degree of doneness, basting kabobs often with reserved marinade. Serve with rice.

Kabobs with a Kick

These colorful kabobs get a flavor boost from a marinade that's ideal for steak—or even chicken. A big plus is that you won't have a lot of pots to clean because you can cook everything at the same time!

Smothered Beef and Peppers

6 to 8 servings

1   cup sliced fresh mushrooms
1   red or green bell pepper, cut into
        strips
2   onions, sliced
1   to 2 tablespoons vegetable oil

2   pounds beef round steak, cut into
        ½" strips
1   (10¾-ounce) can cream of
        mushroom soup, undiluted
⅔   cup water
¾   cup dry red wine or beef broth

1   teaspoon salt
1   teaspoon pepper
2   teaspoons browning-and-seasoning
        sauce (optional)
Hot cooked rice

1 Cook first 3 ingredients in hot oil in a large skillet, stirring constantly, until tender; remove vegetables from skillet, reserving drippings in skillet.

2 Brown steak in reserved drippings, stirring often. Combine soup, water, and wine; pour over steak. Cover and simmer 15 minutes, stirring often.

3 Stir salt and pepper into mushroom mixture; spoon over steak. Cover and simmer 1 hour or until steak is tender, stirring occasionally; stir in browning-and-seasoning sauce, if desired. Serve over rice.

" You can get rich quick with this recipe—a richer color, that is! Just use browning-and-seasoning sauce—it gives this dish its rich brown color. "

Tangy Short Ribs and Vegetables

4 servings

3   pounds lean beef short ribs
3   tablespoons vegetable oil

4   medium baking potatoes, unpeeled
      and quartered (about 2 pounds)
4   carrots, peeled and cut into
      2" pieces
1   medium onion, sliced

1   (14½-ounce) can beef broth,
      divided
2   tablespoons white vinegar
2   tablespoons ketchup
1   tablespoon prepared horseradish
1   tablespoon prepared mustard
1   teaspoon salt
¼   teaspoon pepper

¼   cup all-purpose flour

1 Brown ribs in hot oil in a large skillet 5 to 6 minutes on each side; drain.

2 Place potatoes, carrot pieces, and onion slices in a 5-quart electric slow cooker, and arrange ribs over vegetables.

3 Combine 1 cup broth, the vinegar, and next 5 ingredients; pour mixture over ribs and vegetables. Cover and chill remaining broth.

4 Cover and cook on HIGH setting 3 to 3½ hours; or cook on HIGH setting 1 hour, reduce heat to LOW, and cook 7 more hours or until ribs are tender. Remove ribs and vegetables, reserving liquid in slow cooker. Keep ribs and vegetables warm.

5 Combine remaining chilled beef broth and flour, stirring until smooth; stir into reserved liquid in slow cooker. Cook on HIGH setting, uncovered, 10 minutes or until thickened, stirring often. Serve with ribs and vegetables.

Great Steak Fajitas

4 servings

1 (1-pound) flank steak
1 tablespoon ground cumin
1 tablespoon chili powder
½ teaspoon garlic powder
¾ teaspoon salt
½ teaspoon ground black pepper

4 (8") flour tortillas

1½ cups thinly sliced green, red, or
      yellow bell pepper
2 small onions, sliced
1 tablespoon vegetable oil
1 tablespoon lime juice

½ cup salsa verde (tomatillo salsa) or
      salsa
¼ cup sour cream

1 Cut steak diagonally across grain into thin strips. Combine cumin and next 4 ingredients in a large heavy-duty, zip-top plastic bag; add steak. Seal and shake to coat.

2 Heat tortillas according to package directions; keep warm.

3 Remove steak from plastic bag, discarding seasoning mixture. Cook steak, pepper slices, and onions in hot oil in a large skillet 6 minutes, stirring constantly, or until steak is done. Remove from heat; stir in lime juice.

4 Spoon meat mixture evenly down center of tortillas, and fold up. Serve with salsa verde and sour cream.

Try 'em with Chicken, Too!

Chicken Fajitas: Substitute 4 skinless, boneless chicken breast halves, cut into strips, for flank steak. Heat 2 tablespoons oil in a heavy skillet. Add chicken, and cook 2 to 3 minutes, stirring constantly. Add peppers and onions, and proceed with Step 3, cooking until chicken is done and vegetables are crisp-tender.

Slow-Cooker Barbecue Sandwiches

6 servings

1   (2½-pound) boneless chuck roast, trimmed
2   medium onions, chopped

1   (12-ounce) can cola-flavored beverage (1½ cups)
⅓   cup Worcestershire sauce
1½ tablespoons apple cider vinegar or white vinegar
1½ teaspoons beef bouillon granules
¾   teaspoon dry mustard
¾   teaspoon chili powder
¼   to ½ teaspoon ground red pepper
3   cloves garlic, minced

1   cup ketchup
1   tablespoon butter
6   hamburger buns

1 Place roast in a 3½- or 4-quart electric slow cooker; add onions.

2 Combine cola and next 7 ingredients; reserve 1 cup sauce, and cover and chill. Pour remaining sauce over roast. Cover and cook on HIGH setting 6 hours; or cook on HIGH 1 hour, reduce heat to LOW, and cook 8 more hours or until roast is very tender.

3 Remove roast and chopped onions from cooker, using a slotted spoon; shred meat with two forks. (Reserve remaining meat juices to spoon over mashed potatoes or toast, if desired.)

4 Combine reserved 1 cup sauce, ketchup, butter, and shredded meat in slow cooker; cook on HIGH setting until thoroughly heated, stirring often. Spoon meat mixture onto buns.

Stroganoff Casserole

(pictured on page 3)
6 to 8 servings

12   ounces wide egg noodles

1   pound ground chuck
1   small onion, chopped
1   green bell pepper, chopped
2   celery ribs, chopped

½   cup beef broth
1   (6-ounce) can tomato paste
1   (4-ounce) can sliced mushrooms,
        drained
½   teaspoon dried oregano

1   (8-ounce) container sour cream
1   (12-ounce) container small-curd
        cottage cheese
1   teaspoon garlic salt
2   cups (8 ounces) shredded
        mozzarella cheese
½   cup grated Parmesan cheese

1 Cook noodles according to package directions; drain and keep warm.

2 Meanwhile, cook ground chuck in a large skillet, stirring until it crumbles and is no longer pink. Drain and return to skillet. Stir in onion, bell pepper, and celery. Cover and cook over medium-high heat 15 minutes or until vegetables are tender, stirring occasionally.

3 Stir in beef broth and next 3 ingredients; set aside.

4 Preheat the oven to 350°. Combine sour cream, cottage cheese, and garlic salt. Add noodles, tossing to coat. Spread half of noodle mixture in a lightly greased 9" x 13" baking dish. Top with half of meat mixture, half of mozzarella cheese, and half of Parmesan cheese. Repeat layers with remaining noodle and meat mixtures.

5 Cover; bake at 350° for 20 minutes. Sprinkle with remaining cheeses, and bake, uncovered, 10 more minutes.

❝I think of this casserole as comfort food at its best—it has hearty, hearty, hearty written all over it! Make it ahead for hectic weeknights. Then just toss a bag of salad greens with your favorite dressing, and supper's on the table!❞

No-Fuss Salisbury Steak

4 servings

1   pound ground beef
¼   cup finely chopped onion
3   tablespoons fine, dry breadcrumbs
      (store-bought)
½   teaspoon salt
½   teaspoon pepper

1   (8-ounce) package sliced fresh
      mushrooms
1   small onion, thinly sliced and
      separated into rings
1   (14.5-ounce) can beef broth
2   tablespoons Worcestershire sauce

2   tablespoons water
1   tablespoon cornstarch

1 Combine first 5 ingredients in a bowl; stir well. Shape mixture into 4 patties.

2 Cook patties in a large skillet over medium heat 5 minutes on each side. Remove patties from skillet, reserving 1 tablespoon drippings in skillet. Set patties aside.

3 Cook mushrooms and onion in drippings over medium-high heat, stirring constantly, 5 minutes or until tender. Add broth and Worcestershire sauce to skillet. Return patties to skillet; bring to a boil. Cover, reduce heat, and simmer 15 minutes. Remove patties from skillet with a slotted spoon; place on a platter. Set aside, and keep warm.

4 Combine water and cornstarch; stir well. Add to broth mixture. Bring to a boil; cook, stirring constantly, 1 minute or until thickened. Spoon over patties.

" If you want to cut this recipe's fat, calories, and sodium by a third, try my secret tricks: Use ground round instead of ground beef, and substitute no-salt-added beef broth and low-sodium Worcestershire sauce for their regular-sodium counterparts. But shhh . . . don't tell! It still tastes so great, I'll betcha your family will never even notice!"

Ground Beef Calzones

8 calzones

1   (3.5-ounce) package pepperoni
     slices

½   pound ground chuck
1   medium onion, chopped
1   clove garlic, minced
1   (6-ounce) can Italian-style or
     regular tomato paste
¼   cup dry red wine or beef broth
¼   teaspoon salt
¼   teaspoon pepper
½   cup grated Parmesan cheese
1   cup (4 ounces) shredded
     mozzarella cheese

1   large egg, lightly beaten
2   tablespoons milk

2   (10-ounce) cans refrigerated
     pizza crust

1 Preheat the oven to 350°. Cut pepperoni slices in half, and set aside.

2 Cook ground chuck, onion, and garlic in a large nonstick skillet, stirring until meat crumbles; drain. Stir in tomato paste and next 3 ingredients; cook 5 minutes, stirring often. Remove from heat; stir in pepperoni and cheeses.

3 Combine egg and milk, stirring well; set aside.

4 Unroll pizza crusts, and cut each into 4 squares. Spoon ⅓ cup meat mixture onto each square, leaving a 1" border around edges; brush edges lightly with egg mixture. Fold crusts in half diagonally. Press edges together to seal, using tines of a fork.

5 Place on a lightly greased baking sheet; brush tops of calzones with egg mixture. Bake at 350° for 20 minutes or until lightly browned.

Cheeseburger Pizza

4 servings

1   pound ground chuck
1   medium onion, chopped
2   cloves garlic, minced
2   teaspoons Worcestershire sauce

2   tablespoons ketchup
2   tablespoons prepared mustard
1   (10-ounce) thin crust prepared
      pizza shell
2   cups (8 ounces) shredded colby-
      Monterey Jack cheese blend
Toppings: shredded lettuce, chopped
      tomatoes, pickle slices

1 Preheat the oven to 450°. Cook first 3 ingredients in a large skillet, stirring until meat crumbles; drain. Stir in Worcestershire sauce.

2 Combine ketchup and mustard, and spread over pizza shell; sprinkle with 1 cup cheese. Top with beef mixture and remaining 1 cup cheese. Bake at 450° for 8 to 10 minutes. Sprinkle with desired toppings.

Yum! An American Original

Forget the fast food joints—try this easy recipe instead. When your family can't decide between burgers and pizza, you'll know what to serve!

Taco Burgers

(pictured on back cover)

4 servings

1 pound ground chuck
1 (1¼-ounce) envelope taco
    seasoning mix

1 cup salsa, divided
1 cup refried beans
3 tablespoons chopped fresh cilantro
4 large hamburger buns

1 medium tomato, diced
1 cup shredded iceberg lettuce
1 small purple onion, sliced
1 cup (4 ounces) shredded zesty
    Mexican cheese or Cheddar
    cheese
Garnish: fresh cilantro sprigs

1 Combine beef and taco seasoning mix; shape into 4 patties. Cook in a large nonstick skillet coated with non-stick cooking spray over medium heat 4 to 5 minutes on each side or until done.

2 Combine ¼ cup salsa, the beans, and cilantro; spread on cut sides of buns.

3 Stir together remaining ¾ cup salsa and the tomato. Serve patties on buns with salsa mixture, lettuce, onion, and cheese. Garnish, if desired.

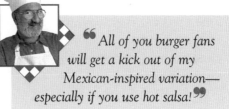

❝ All of you burger fans will get a kick out of my Mexican-inspired variation— especially if you use hot salsa! ❞

Chicken with White Barbecue Sauce

4 servings

1½ cups mayonnaise
⅓ cup apple cider vinegar
¼ cup lemon juice
2 tablespoons sugar
2 tablespoons freshly ground pepper
2 tablespoons white wine Worcestershire sauce

4 chicken leg quarters

1 Combine first 6 ingredients in a small bowl; stir well.

2 Place chicken in a large heavy-duty, zip-top plastic bag; pour ¾ cup sauce over chicken, turning to coat. Seal bag, and marinate in refrigerator 8 hours, turning bag occasionally. Cover and chill remaining sauce.

3 Remove chicken, discarding marinade; arrange chicken in a 7" x 11" microwave-safe dish with skin side down and thicker portion of chicken toward outside of dish. Cover with wax paper, and microwave at HIGH setting 5 minutes; turn and rearrange chicken. Microwave 5 to 6 more minutes.

4 Preheat the grill. Grill chicken, skin side up and uncovered, over medium-hot coals (350° to 400°) 15 to 20 minutes or until done, turning once and basting with half of reserved sauce. (See box at left.) Serve with remaining reserved sauce.

Safe Serving

Set aside some of the tangy white barbecue sauce before basting. Then serve it alongside the chicken. That way, there's no risk of the table sauce having any bacteria transferred via the basting brush!

A Chicken in Every Pot

4 servings

2 ½ pounds assorted chicken pieces, skinned, if desired
1 teaspoon paprika
¼ teaspoon salt
½ teaspoon ground black pepper
1 tablespoon vegetable oil

1 ½ cups long-grain rice, uncooked
2 cloves garlic, minced
1 (14-ounce) can chicken broth
1 (14½-ounce) can diced tomatoes, undrained
1 green bell pepper, cut into thin strips

1 ½ cups frozen English peas

1 Sprinkle chicken with paprika, salt, and black pepper. Heat oil in an ovenproof Dutch oven over medium-high heat until hot. Add chicken to Dutch oven; cook on all sides until browned. Remove chicken from Dutch oven, and set aside.

2 Preheat the oven to 350°. Add rice and garlic to Dutch oven. Cook over medium-high heat, stirring constantly, 1 minute. Add chicken broth, tomatoes, and green pepper. Bring to a boil over high heat, stirring once. Return chicken to Dutch oven.

3 Cover and bake at 350° for 40 minutes. Stir in peas; cover and let stand 5 minutes.

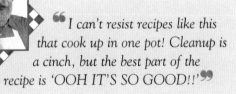

“ I can't resist recipes like this that cook up in one pot! Cleanup is a cinch, but the best part of the recipe is ‘OOH IT'S SO GOOD!!’ ”

Delicious Drumsticks

5 servings

1   cup fine, dry breadcrumbs
       (store-bought)
2¼   teaspoons onion powder
2¼   teaspoons curry powder
¾   teaspoon garlic powder
¾   teaspoon dry mustard
¾   teaspoon paprika
¼   teaspoon ground red pepper
1   teaspoon salt

3   pounds chicken legs
½   cup butter, melted

1 Preheat the oven to 350°. Combine first 8 ingredients on a plate; stir well.

2 Place chicken in a large bowl. Drizzle evenly with butter; dredge in bread-crumb mixture.

3 Place chicken on an aluminum foil-lined broiler pan. Bake, uncovered, at 350° for 1 hour and 15 minutes or until chicken is done, turning chicken occasionally.

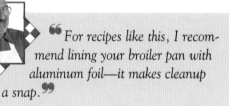

For recipes like this, I recommend lining your broiler pan with aluminum foil—it makes cleanup a snap.

Chicken Thighs Cacciatore

4 servings

8	chicken thighs, skinned, if desired
¼	teaspoon salt
¼	teaspoon pepper
2	tablespoons olive oil, divided
½	cup chopped onion
2	cloves garlic, minced
½	cup dry red wine or beef broth
2	(14½-ounce) cans diced Italian-style tomatoes, undrained

1 Sprinkle chicken with salt and pepper. Cook chicken in 1 tablespoon olive oil in a large heavy skillet over medium-high heat 3 minutes on each side or until lightly browned. Remove from skillet, and set aside.

2 Cook onion and garlic in skillet in remaining 1 tablespoon oil, stirring constantly, until tender.

3 Add chicken, wine, and tomatoes. Bring to a boil. Cover, reduce heat, and simmer 10 minutes. Uncover and simmer 10 more minutes.

Catchy Name

"Cacciatore" is Italian for hunter. And this chicken recipe is prepared "hunter style" with tomatoes, onions, herbs, and wine.

Southwestern Chicken and Rice

4 servings

1   (1¼-ounce) package taco
    seasoning mix
4   skinned and boned chicken breast
    halves

1   cup salsa
2   cups water

2   cups uncooked instant rice
1   cup canned black beans, rinsed and
    drained
1   cup (4 ounces) shredded Mexican
    cheese blend
Sour cream

1 Rub 1 tablespoon taco seasoning mix on chicken.

2 Combine remaining taco seasoning mix, salsa, and water in a large skillet; top mixture with chicken. Bring to a boil; cover, reduce heat, and simmer 10 minutes or until chicken is done. Remove chicken from skillet.

3 Stir in rice, beans, and cheese; cover and cook over low heat 5 minutes. Top with chicken. Serve with sour cream.

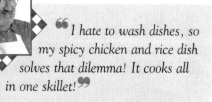

❝ I hate to wash dishes, so my spicy chicken and rice dish solves that dilemma! It cooks all in one skillet! ❞

Chow Mein Chicken Casserole

6 servings

1 tablespoon butter
1 small red bell pepper, chopped
2 cloves garlic, minced
2 (8-ounce) packages sliced fresh
    mushrooms

3 green onions, chopped
1 (10¾-ounce) can cream of
    mushroom soup, undiluted
¾ cup mayonnaise
1 tablespoon soy sauce
3 cups chopped cooked chicken
¼ teaspoon black pepper

½ (5-ounce) can chow mein noodles
    (2 cups)

1 Preheat the oven to 350°. Melt butter in a large skillet. Add red bell pepper, garlic, and mushrooms; sauté until tender.

2 Stir in chopped green onions and next 5 ingredients.

3 Pour into a lightly greased 7" x 11" baking dish. Sprinkle with chow mein noodles. Bake, uncovered, at 350° for 30 minutes or until bubbly.

Substitution Savvy

Don't worry if you don't have the exact ingredients on hand. You can substitute green bell pepper for the red, cream of chicken soup for mushroom soup, and chopped cooked pork for the chicken. And if you have canned mushrooms in your pantry, 2 (4.5-ounce) cans substitute nicely for the fresh. Just drain 'em—there's no need to sauté!

Chicken-Almond Stir-Fry

4 servings

2   tablespoons sesame or vegetable oil

4   skinned and boned chicken breast
     halves, cut into thin strips
1   (2.25-ounce) package sliced
     almonds
1   (16-ounce) package frozen broccoli,
     carrots, and water chestnuts

1   tablespoon cornstarch
1   tablespoon brown sugar
½   teaspoon ground ginger
½   cup soy sauce
⅓   cup pineapple juice
Hot cooked rice

1 Pour oil around top of a preheated wok, coating sides, or in a large nonstick skillet. Heat briefly at medium-high (375°).

2 Add chicken and almonds; cook, stirring constantly, 2 minutes. Add frozen vegetables; cover and cook 4 minutes, stirring once.

3 Combine cornstarch and next 4 ingredients; add to wok. Cook, stirring constantly, 2 to 3 minutes or until mixture thickens. Serve over rice.

❝Need dinner on the table in less than 20 minutes? Try my saucy chicken recipe—because it's a stir-fry, it'll be done by the time the rice is ready! Stir-frying cooks food in a small amount of oil over high heat with constant stirring. Make sure the chicken strips are uniform in shape and size. Then the chicken will cook evenly and in the same length of time as the vegetables.❞

Slow-Cooker Chicken Lasagna Florentine

4 to 6 servings

1 (10-ounce) package frozen chopped spinach, thawed

1 (9-ounce) package frozen diced cooked chicken
2 (10¾-ounce) cans cream of chicken soup, undiluted
1 (8-ounce) carton sour cream
1 cup freshly grated Parmesan cheese
1 cup milk
⅓ cup chopped onion
⅓ cup mayonnaise
½ teaspoon salt
¼ teaspoon ground nutmeg

9 lasagna noodles, uncooked
3 cups (12 ounces) shredded mozzarella cheese

1 Press spinach between layers of paper towels to remove excess moisture.

2 Combine spinach, chicken, and next 8 ingredients in a large bowl; stir mixture well.

3 Place 3 uncooked noodles in bottom of a lightly greased 5-quart electric slow cooker, breaking noodles in half as necessary to fit in slow cooker. Spread one-third of chicken mixture over noodles; sprinkle with 1 cup mozzarella cheese. Layer with 3 more noodles, half of remaining chicken mixture, and 1 cup cheese. Layer remaining noodles and chicken mixture over cheese; sprinkle with remaining 1 cup cheese.

4 Cover and cook on HIGH setting 1 hour. Reduce heat to LOW, and cook 5 more hours.

Turkey Picante

6 servings

1   (8-ounce) package shredded
      Mexican cheese blend, divided
1   (1¼-ounce) envelope taco
      seasoning mix, divided
¾   cup yellow cornmeal
1   large egg
⅓   cup milk
6   turkey cutlets (about 1 pound)

2   tablespoons vegetable oil

1   (16-ounce) jar picante sauce
¼   cup chopped fresh cilantro
1   cup water

Hot Mexican rice (store-bought)
Garnish: fresh cilantro sprigs

1 Combine 1 cup cheese, 2 tablespoons taco seasoning mix, the cornmeal, egg, and milk. Rub or press cornmeal mixture onto both sides of cutlets. (The cornmeal mixture will be thick like a paste.)

2 Cook 3 turkey cutlets in 1 tablespoon hot oil in a large nonstick skillet over medium-high heat 2 to 3 minutes on each side or until golden. Repeat with remaining cutlets and oil. Remove from skillet.

3 Combine remaining 1 cup cheese, remaining taco seasoning mix, the picante sauce, chopped cilantro, and 1 cup water in skillet. Place turkey over sauce mixture; cover and cook over medium heat 5 minutes or until thoroughly heated.

4 Serve turkey over Mexican rice, and spoon remaining sauce over turkey. Garnish, if desired.

Southwestern Pork Chops

4 servings

4   (½"-thick) boneless pork chops
¼   cup (1 ounce) shredded Mexican
     cheese blend
¼   cup fine, dry breadcrumbs
     (store-bought)
2   tablespoons milk

2   tablespoons vegetable oil, divided

2   cloves garlic, minced
1   small onion, chopped
2   (15¼-ounce) cans whole kernel corn
     with red and green peppers,
     rinsed and drained
¼   cup chopped fresh cilantro

1   tablespoon lime juice

1 Place pork chops between two sheets of heavy-duty plastic wrap, and flatten to ¼" thickness, using a meat mallet or rolling pin. Combine cheese and breadcrumbs. Dip pork chops in milk, and dredge in breadcrumb mixture.

2 Brown chops in 1 tablespoon hot oil in a large nonstick skillet over medium-high heat 3 minutes on each side. Remove from skillet.

3 Cook garlic and onion in remaining 1 tablespoon hot oil in skillet, stirring constantly, until tender. Stir in corn and cilantro. Cook 2 to 3 minutes, stirring often.

4 Top with pork, and drizzle with lime juice. Cover and cook over medium heat 7 minutes or until pork is done.

❝I bet you're gonna want to try my Italian version of these tender pork chops, too! Just substitute 6-cheese Italian blend for Mexican, Italian-seasoned breadcrumbs for plain, fresh parsley for the cilantro, and lemon juice for the lime juice. Perfecto!❞

Pork Chops and Gravy

6 servings

¾ cup all-purpose flour
1½ teaspoons dry mustard
½ teaspoon garlic powder
½ teaspoon salt
½ teaspoon pepper
6 (1"-thick) lean pork chops

2 tablespoons vegetable oil
1 (14-ounce) can chicken broth

¼ cup water

1 Combine first 5 ingredients, stirring until blended. Set aside ⅓ cup flour mixture for gravy. Trim excess fat from pork chops, if needed. Dredge pork chops in remaining flour mixture, and set aside.

2 Pour oil into a large skillet; place over medium-high heat until hot. Cook chops in hot oil, in batches, just until browned on both sides; place in a 4½-quart slow cooker. Pour broth over chops. Cover and cook on HIGH setting 2½ hours or until chops are tender.

3 Remove pork chops from slow cooker, and arrange over hot cooked rice or mashed potatoes; keep warm. Combine water and reserved ⅓ cup flour mixture, stirring until blended. Whisk flour mixture into juices in slow cooker until blended. Cook on HIGH, uncovered, 10 minutes or until thickened, stirring occasionally. Spoon gravy over pork chops, and sprinkle with additional pepper.

Grilled Brats with Onion Relish

8 servings

8   fresh bratwurst (about 2 pounds)
1   (12-ounce) can beer or 1½ cups
      water

8   hoagie rolls or French bread rolls
Onion Relish

1 Combine bratwurst and beer in a Dutch oven. Bring almost to a boil; reduce heat, and simmer, uncovered, 10 minutes. Remove bratwurst from beer.

2 Preheat the grill. Grill bratwurst, uncovered, over medium-hot coals (350° to 400°) 7 to 8 minutes or until done. Serve on rolls with Onion Relish and desired condiments.

Onion Relish

¼   cup vegetable oil
½   cup sugar
1   large onion, chopped
1   (14.5-ounce) can sauerkraut,
      well drained
⅓   cup cider vinegar
½   teaspoon caraway seeds

Heat oil in a skillet over medium heat. Add sugar; cook, stirring constantly, 10 minutes or until sugar turns a light caramel color. Add onion and sauerkraut; simmer, uncovered, over medium heat 20 minutes, stirring often. (Sugar will harden when onion and sauerkraut are added but will dissolve as mixture simmers.) Add vinegar and caraway seeds; simmer, uncovered, 15 minutes. Store, covered, in refrigerator up to 1 week. Yield: 2½ cups.

Bratwurst Basics

This wurst (German for sausage) is a combination of pork and veal seasoned with a variety of spices, including caraway, marjoram, ginger, and nutmeg. Boil brats first to cook them thoroughly and to keep them plump when grilled.

Sausage-Stuffed French Loaf

8 servings

1   (16-ounce) loaf French bread

1   pound ground pork sausage
1   medium onion, chopped
1   cup (4 ounces) shredded
        mozzarella cheese
¼   cup chopped fresh parsley
1   teaspoon Dijon mustard
¼   teaspoon fennel seeds
¼   teaspoon salt
¼   teaspoon pepper
1   large egg, lightly beaten

2   tablespoons butter
1   clove garlic, minced

" I like to serve this versatile loaf alongside a big salad or creamy soup. But you can also slice it thinly for appetizers for the big game. Or cut it into hearty sandwiches, and you've got enough for a meal! If you prefer bold flavors (like I do!), use spicy sausage. "

1 Preheat the oven to 400°. Cut off ends of French bread loaf, and set ends aside. Hollow out the center of loaf with a long serrated bread knife, leaving a ½"-thick shell. Position knife blade in food processor bowl; add bread removed from inside the loaf. Process to make coarse crumbs. Set bread shell and crumbs aside.

2 Cook sausage and onion in a skillet until sausage is browned, stirring until it crumbles; drain well. Stir in 1 cup reserved bread crumbs, the cheese, and next 6 ingredients. Spoon sausage mixture into bread shell. Replace loaf ends, securing with toothpicks (they keep the sausage mixture from coming out of the loaf during baking).

3 Melt butter in a small saucepan; add garlic, and cook about 1 minute. Brush over loaf. Wrap loaf in aluminum foil, leaving open slightly on top.

4 Bake at 400° for 20 minutes or until cheese thoroughly melts. Cut into 8 slices.

Super Sideshow

"Round out your meals with these versatile side dishes. They're so tasty, you may be tempted to make 'em the main course!"

Ranch-Style Baked Beans

8 servings

½   pound ground chuck
½   cup chopped onion

1½ cups hickory-flavored barbecue
     sauce
⅓   cup firmly packed brown sugar
1   (15-ounce) can kidney beans,
     drained
1   (15.5-ounce) can butter beans,
     drained
1   (16-ounce) can pork and beans,
     undrained
10 slices bacon, cooked and crumbled

1 Preheat the oven to 350°. Cook beef and onion in a Dutch oven, stirring until meat crumbles; drain and place in a large bowl.

2 Stir barbecue sauce and remaining ingredients into beef mixture. Spoon mixture into a lightly greased 2½-quart baking dish.

3 Bake, uncovered, at 350° for 1 hour, stirring beans once.

Round 'em Up!
Corral your family—it's chow time! Your favorite hickory-flavored barbecue sauce and ground chuck give three different kinds of beans lots of flavor!

Tomato-Feta Green Beans

6 servings

¼ cup pine nuts or walnuts

2 (16-ounce) packages frozen
    French-style green beans,
    thawed

2 cloves garlic, minced
2 teaspoons dried Italian seasoning
1 tablespoon olive oil

4 plum tomatoes, chopped
2 tablespoons lemon juice
1 teaspoon salt
½ teaspoon pepper
1 (4-ounce) package crumbled feta
    cheese

1 Preheat the oven to 350°. Bake pine nuts in a shallow pan at 350° for 6 to 8 minutes or until toasted. Set aside.

2 Meanwhile, drain green beans well, pressing between layers of paper towels.

3 Cook garlic and Italian seasoning in hot oil in a large skillet over medium heat, stirring constantly, 1 minute; add green beans. Cook, stirring constantly, 5 to 7 minutes.

4 Stir in tomatoes. Cook, stirring constantly, 2 minutes or until mixture is thoroughly heated. Stir in lemon juice, salt, and pepper. Sprinkle with cheese and pine nuts.

Spicy Orange Beets

4 to 6 servings

2   pounds small fresh beets

¼   cup firmly packed brown sugar
2   teaspoons cornstarch
¼   teaspoon ground allspice
¼   teaspoon salt
⅛   teaspoon pepper
⅔   cup orange juice
2   tablespoons butter

1   tablespoon chopped fresh chives

1 Leave root and 1" of stem on beets; scrub with a vegetable brush. Place beets in a saucepan, and cover with water. Cook beets over medium-high heat 30 minutes or until tender. Drain. Pour cold water over beets, and drain. Trim roots and stems, and rub off skins. Cut beets into ¼" slices; set aside.

2 Combine brown sugar and next 4 ingredients in a large saucepan; gradually add orange juice, stirring mixture until smooth. Stir in butter; bring to a boil, stirring constantly. Boil, stirring constantly, 1 minute.

3 Add beets; cook until thoroughly heated. Sprinkle with chives before serving.

"Beet" the Clock

Ever cooked beets from scratch? This recipe walks you through the method, step-by-step. But if you wanna get your side dish on the table in less than 10 minutes, you can substitute 2 (14½-ounce) cans of sliced, drained beets for fresh, and omit Step 1. Proceed with Step 2.

Broccoli Casserole

6 to 8 servings

2 (10-ounce) packages frozen
  chopped broccoli, thawed

1 (10¾-ounce) can cream of
  mushroom soup, undiluted
1 cup (4 ounces) shredded sharp
  Cheddar cheese
¼ cup mayonnaise
2 large eggs, lightly beaten
1 teaspoon grated onion

¾ cup cheese cracker crumbs

1 Preheat the oven to 350°. Press thawed broccoli between paper towels to remove excess moisture.

2 Combine broccoli, cream of mushroom soup, and next 4 ingredients. Spoon into a greased 2-quart casserole.

3 Top casserole with cracker crumbs. Bake at 350° for 30 minutes.

66 I've spruced up this family favorite by putting just a few extra minutes into the crumb topping and garnish. Remember, it's the little things that count! If you're entertaining, sprinkle the cracker crumbs in a design on top. For instance, to make diagonal rows of breadcrumbs, cut 1½"-wide strips of wax paper and lay them in rows before sprinkling the crumbs to get a uniform look—simple! 99

Brussels Sprouts in Cashew Sauce

4 servings

1½ pounds fresh brussels sprouts or
    2 (10-ounce) packages frozen
    brussels sprouts

⅓ cup butter
1 tablespoon brown sugar
3 tablespoons soy sauce
2 teaspoons white vinegar
¼ teaspoon pepper
¼ teaspoon minced garlic

⅓ cup cashews

1 If using fresh brussels sprouts, wash thoroughly; remove any discolored leaves. Cut off stem ends, and slash bottom of each sprout with a shallow X.

2 Place fresh or frozen brussels sprouts in a large saucepan; add water to cover. Bring to a boil. Reduce heat, and cook 10 minutes or until tender. Drain well; set aside.

3 Melt butter in a small skillet over medium heat; add brown sugar and next 4 ingredients. Bring to a boil, stirring constantly; remove from heat.

4 Stir cashews into butter sauce. Pour sauce over brussels sprouts. Serve immediately.

Give It a Blue Ribbon!

This brussels sprouts recipe is a definite winner—it'll reel in so many compliments, it oughta have a blue ribbon on it! Glazed with a sweet cashew sauce, the brussels sprouts will have your gang coming back for seconds!

Sautéed Carrots and Zucchini

6 servings

2	tablespoons butter or margarine
1	pound carrots, peeled and thinly sliced
¼	cup chopped green onions (white part only)
1	pound zucchini, thinly sliced
¼	teaspoon salt
¼	teaspoon freshly ground pepper
3	tablespoons chopped fresh basil or 1 teaspoon dried basil

1 Melt butter in a large skillet over medium-high heat. Add carrot; cook, uncovered, 4 minutes, stirring often.

2 Add green onions, and cook 1 more minute. Add zucchini, and cook 2 more minutes, stirring occasionally.

3 Stir in salt and pepper; cover, reduce heat to medium-low, and cook 4 minutes or until crisp-tender. Sprinkle with basil.

Cauliflower Bake

6 servings

1   large cauliflower, cut into florets
½   teaspoon salt
3   cups water

¼   cup butter, melted
½   teaspoon salt
½   teaspoon ground black pepper
1   cup round buttery cracker crumbs
        (about 23 crackers)
1½ cups (6 ounces) shredded Cheddar
        cheese, divided
1   medium onion, chopped
½   cup chopped green bell pepper
1   (16-ounce) can diced tomatoes,
        undrained

1 Preheat the oven to 350°. Combine first 3 ingredients in a large saucepan; bring to a boil. Cover, reduce heat, and cook 5 minutes or until tender; drain. Set aside.

2 Combine butter and next 3 ingredients in a large bowl; stir in cauliflower, 1 cup cheese, the onion, bell pepper, and tomatoes. Spoon into a lightly greased 9" x 13" baking dish.

3 Bake at 350° for 35 minutes. Sprinkle with remaining ½ cup cheese, and bake 5 more minutes.

Cauliflower Acclaim
Cauliflower never tasted—or looked—better! It'll perform beautifully with any star attraction—roast beef, chicken, or turkey.

Sweet-and-Hot Onion Rings

6 servings

3   cups buttermilk biscuit mix
1   tablespoon ground red pepper
1   (14-ounce) can sweetened
      condensed milk
½   cup club soda

Vegetable oil

2   large yellow onions, cut into ¼"
      slices and separated into rings

1 Combine biscuit mix and red pepper in a medium bowl; stir in condensed milk and club soda.

2 Pour oil to depth of 3" into a Dutch oven; heat to 375°.

3 Dip onion rings into batter, coating well; fry, a few at a time, in hot oil until golden brown. Drain onion rings on paper towels. Serve immediately.

"You can have onion rings just like you'd get at your favorite hamburger joint—and you don't even have to leave your house! Sweetened condensed milk and club soda are my secret ingredients! The effervescence of club soda activates the leavening agents in the biscuit mix for a puffy coating on my delicious onion rings."

Creole Black-Eyed Peas

10 servings

1   pound smoked sausage, sliced

3   medium onions, chopped
1   medium-size green bell pepper, chopped
4   cloves garlic, minced

3   (15.5-ounce) cans fresh shelled black-eyed peas
1   (8-ounce) can tomato sauce
1   ham-flavored bouillon cube
½   to 1 teaspoon ground red pepper
1   teaspoon ground black pepper
1   cup chopped fresh parsley

1 Brown sausage in a Dutch oven over medium heat, stirring occasionally. Remove from Dutch oven.

2 Sauté onions, bell pepper, and garlic in Dutch oven until tender.

3 Stir in sausage, peas, and next 4 ingredients; cook until thoroughly heated, stirring often. Stir in parsley.

Did You Know?
Black-eyed peas (also known as cowpeas) are not really peas at all; they're black pigmented lentils. The custom of eating them on New Year's Day for luck dates back to the Egyptian pharaohs.

Dill-icious Peas

4 servings

1   (16-ounce) package frozen
     English peas

¼   cup mayonnaise
¼   cup light sour cream
1½ tablespoons prepared horseradish
1½ tablespoons Dijon mustard
2   tablespoons chopped fresh dill or
     2 teaspoons dried dillweed
⅛   teaspoon coarsely ground pepper

1 Cook peas according to package directions; drain and cool.

2 Combine mayonnaise and next 5 ingredients; stir well. Add to peas, stirring gently. Cover and chill at least 2 hours.

"I used to serve peas with only a pat of butter melted on top. No more! My easy creamy dill sauce makes them so-o-o special!"

Cheesy Onion Potatoes

6 servings

6	medium baking potatoes, unpeeled and cubed (about 2 pounds)
¼	cup butter
1	(1-ounce) envelope onion soup mix
1½	cups (6 ounces) shredded Cheddar cheese
5	green onions, chopped

1 Preheat the oven to 400°. Place potatoes in a 9" x 13" baking dish coated with nonstick cooking spray. Dot with butter, and sprinkle dry onion soup mix over the top.

2 Cover and bake at 400° for 25 minutes; uncover and stir. Cover and bake 30 more minutes. Sprinkle with cheese and green onions; serve immediately.

" These home-style potatoes topped with Cheddar cheese bring back memories of a restaurant specialty. A scrumptious side dish couldn't be any easier! My recipe calls for unpeeled potatoes, which make this dish quick. Remember, though, there are no rules. So if you want to peel your potatoes, go for it!"

Rosemary Potatoes au Gratin

6 servings

4 medium baking potatoes, peeled and thinly sliced (about 1½ pounds)

1½ cups milk
1 (15/16-ounce) envelope chicken gravy mix

1 teaspoon dried rosemary, crushed
¼ teaspoon pepper
3 tablespoons grated Parmesan cheese

1 Preheat the oven to 400°. Arrange potato slices in a lightly greased 7" x 11" baking dish.

2 Combine milk and gravy mix; pour over potato slices.

3 Sprinkle potatoes with rosemary, pepper, and Parmesan cheese. Bake at 400° for 35 to 40 minutes or until potatoes are tender.

You Say Potato . . .

There's a lot to love about potatoes: They're rich in vitamins and minerals, and they're virtually fat free. If you're looking for a good baking potato, try Russet. Best known as the Idaho potato, the Russet's mealy texture is good for baking and mashing, and making scalloped or au gratin dishes like this one!

Bacon-Walnut Spinach

2 servings

4   slices bacon

2½ tablespoons white wine vinegar

1   (10-ounce) package fresh spinach
2   tablespoons chopped walnuts
¼   teaspoon pepper
Pinch of sugar (optional)

1 Cook bacon in a large skillet until crisp; remove bacon, reserving 1 tablespoon drippings in skillet. Crumble bacon, and set aside.

2 Add vinegar to skillet; bring to a boil over medium-high heat, stirring to loosen bacon particles that cling to bottom.

3 Add spinach, and cook, stirring constantly, 1 to 2 minutes or until wilted. Stir in bacon, walnuts, pepper, and, if desired, sugar. Serve immediately.

Fresh Start

If packaged fresh spinach is not available, you can substitute a pound of loose fresh spinach leaves. Just wash and trim the leaves, and you're ready to go!

Acorn Squash with Onion-Berry Filling

4 servings

2 medium acorn squash
½ cup water

1 orange

2 cups chopped purple onion
2 tablespoons olive oil
⅓ cup firmly packed brown sugar

1 (16-ounce) can whole-berry
cranberry sauce

1 Cut squash in half, slicing through stem end; scoop out and discard seeds. Place squash, cut sides down, in a 7" x 11" microwave-safe dish. Pour ½ cup water into dish. Cover and microwave at HIGH setting 12 minutes or until tender.

2 Meanwhile, cut unpeeled orange into quarters, and remove seeds. Pulse orange (with rind) in food processor until chopped; set aside.

3 Cook onion in hot oil in a skillet, stirring constantly, 5 minutes or until lightly browned. Stir in brown sugar, and cook 4 more minutes.

4 Remove from heat. Stir in cranberry sauce and chopped orange. Spoon mixture into squash halves, reserving remaining mixture for another use.

Squash, Anyone?

Looking for an elegant side dish for company? This acorn squash is elegant AND easy! The squash family has many members, ranging from ivory to ebony, from petite to gargantuan, and from savory to sugary. Almost all of these, with the exception of spaghetti squash, are interchangeable with the acorn squash in this recipe.

Stir-Fried Squash

(pictured on facing page)
4 to 6 servings

1	tablespoon olive oil
3	cups sliced yellow squash (about 1 pound)
1	sweet onion, coarsely chopped
1	small red bell pepper, sliced
3	cloves garlic, minced
¼	cup water
½	teaspoon salt
¼	teaspoon ground black pepper

1 Pour oil around top of a nonstick wok or large skillet, coating sides; place over medium-high heat (375°) 1 minute. Add squash, onion, and bell pepper.

2 Cook, stirring constantly, 10 to 12 minutes or until vegetables are crisp-tender.

3 Stir in garlic and remaining ingredients. Cook until squash is tender, stirring often. Serve immediately.

"Who can resist fresh squash? Not me! I like to showcase the subtle flavor of garden-fresh summer squash with this easy stir-fry—a great change of pace from the usual casserole. But you can also enjoy the shapely vegetable raw, steamed, baked, grilled, deep-fried, or even pickled!"

Mexican Beef Salad, page 131

Parsley-Garlic Rolls, page 140

Grilled Summer Vegetables

(pictured on facing page)

4 servings

1 medium-size red bell pepper, cut into 6 strips

1 small eggplant (about ½ pound), cut crosswise into ½"-thick slices

1 small zucchini, quartered lengthwise

1 small yellow squash, quartered lengthwise

¼ cup herb vinaigrette or Italian salad dressing

¼ teaspoon salt

1 Preheat the grill. Combine first 5 ingredients, tossing vegetables gently to coat with vinaigrette.

2 Coat grill rack with nonstick cooking spray; place on grill over medium-hot coals (350° to 400°). Place vegetables on rack, and grill, uncovered, 5 minutes on each side or until crisp-tender, turning once. Transfer to a serving platter, and sprinkle with salt.

" If you have picky eaters in your family who never want their veggies, try grilling—it brings out the natural flavors of fresh vegetables. I just brush on a little salad dressing to heighten the flavor, and WOW!! You won't be able to keep those finicky folks away!"

Fettuccine Alfredo

6 servings

12 ounces dried fettuccine, uncooked

1 cup whipping cream
½ cup butter, melted
¾ cup freshly grated Parmesan cheese
2 tablespoons chopped fresh parsley
¼ teaspoon freshly ground pepper

1 Cook pasta according to package directions; drain well.

2 Meanwhile, combine whipping cream and remaining 4 ingredients. Pour cream mixture over hot pasta immediately after draining pasta, and toss gently. Serve immediately.

"Who doesn't love this classic pasta dish with its rich, cheesy sauce? The hot pasta melts the creamy Parmesan cheese for a foolproof side dish. It's even rich enough to serve as a main dish. Just add a salad, some crusty bread, and top off the meal with a glass of wine!"

Lemon Couscous

3 servings

1	cup chicken broth
1	tablespoon grated lemon rind (optional)
2	tablespoons fresh lemon juice
1	tablespoon butter
¼	teaspoon salt
⅔	cup couscous, uncooked
2	tablespoons pecan pieces, toasted
2	tablespoons chopped fresh parsley
1	(2-ounce) jar diced pimiento, drained

1 Combine first 5 ingredients in a saucepan; bring to a boil.

2 Add couscous, stirring well; cover, remove from heat, and let stand 5 minutes.

3 Fluff couscous with a fork. Stir in pecans, parsley, and pimiento.

Move Over, Rice!

Couscous, an ideal side dish with any entrée, is technically a tiny round Middle Eastern pasta. It's so fine, it's often thought of as a grain. Couscous is ready in a flash and absorbs flavors as it soaks up liquid. You can add almost anything to it to tailor it to your entrée. And best of all, it takes mere minutes to make!

Sausage-Rice Dressing

(pictured on page 2)
8 servings

1   (6-ounce) package long-grain-and-
    wild rice mix

1   (4.5-ounce) jar sliced mushrooms,
    undrained

1   pound ground pork sausage
1   large onion, chopped
3   celery ribs, chopped
1   bunch green onions, sliced
1   small green bell pepper, chopped
2   cloves garlic, minced

1   tablespoon all-purpose flour
1   tablespoon Worcestershire sauce
1   teaspoon chicken-flavored bouillon
    granules

1 Cook rice according to package directions, omitting butter. Set aside.

2 Drain mushrooms, reserving liquid; add enough water to mushroom liquid to measure ¾ cup.

3 Cook sausage and next 5 ingredients in a Dutch oven over medium heat, stirring until sausage crumbles. Drain.

4 Stir flour into sausage mixture; cook over medium heat, stirring constantly, 1 minute. Stir in mushrooms, mushroom liquid, Worcestershire sauce, and bouillon granules. Bring mixture to a boil; cover, reduce heat, and simmer 5 minutes. Stir in cooked rice, and cook until thoroughly heated.

Soup and Salad Bar

66These cozy soups and sensational salads taste ooh-so-good, no one will ever believe how easy they are!99

French Onion Soup

2 servings

2 tablespoons butter
2 medium onions, sliced and
    separated into rings

3 cups canned beef broth
1 tablespoon Worcestershire sauce
¼ teaspoon salt
¼ teaspoon pepper

2 (½"-thick) slices French bread
2 tablespoons (½ ounce) shredded
    Swiss cheese

1 Preheat the oven to Broil. Melt butter in a large saucepan. Add onions, and cook, stirring constantly, 2 minutes or until tender.

2 Add broth and next 3 ingredients; bring to a boil. Reduce heat, and simmer, uncovered, 15 minutes.

3 Place bread slices on a baking sheet, and broil 5½" from heat (with electric oven door partially opened) 1 minute or until lightly browned. Turn bread over; sprinkle evenly with cheese. Broil 1 more minute or until cheese melts.

4 To serve, ladle soup into bowls; top each serving with a toasted bread slice. Serve immediately.

66 Who knew this pub favorite could be OOH-SO-EASY?! I like to top it off with a slice of cheese toast. The recipe doubles easily to serve four. 99

Beer-Cheese Soup

4 servings

2½ cups milk
1   (12-ounce) can beer, divided

2   (8-ounce) jars process cheese
        spread
1   (10½-ounce) can condensed
        chicken broth, undiluted
½   teaspoon Worcestershire sauce
2   dashes of hot sauce

3   tablespoons cornstarch

1 Combine milk and ¾ cup beer in a Dutch oven. Cook over medium heat, stirring constantly, until thoroughly heated.

2 Add cheese spread and next 3 ingredients. Cook over low heat, stirring constantly, until thoroughly heated.

3 Combine cornstarch and remaining beer; add to cheese mixture. Simmer, stirring constantly, 10 minutes or until thickened (do not boil).

Grand Garnishes

Warm up to a bowl of this smooth soup, and chase away the winter blues! Top it off with a contrasting crunch: Cook and crumble some bacon or add some chopped green onions. You can even sprinkle the soup with some croutons. Pick your favorite toppings, and it can be a different soup every time!

Taco Soup

8 to 10 servings

1   pound ground chuck
1   large onion, chopped

3   (15½-ounce) cans Mexican-style
     chili beans, undrained
1   (15¼-ounce) can whole kernel corn,
     undrained
1   (15-ounce) can tomato sauce
1   (14½-ounce) can diced tomatoes,
     undrained
1   (4.5-ounce) can chopped green
     chiles, undrained
1   (1¼-ounce) envelope taco
     seasoning mix
1   (1-ounce) envelope Ranch-style
     dressing mix
1½ cups water

Toppings: corn chips, shredded lettuce,
    chopped tomato, sour cream,
    shredded Cheddar cheese

1 Cook beef and onion in a Dutch oven over medium-high heat until meat is browned and onion is tender, stirring until meat crumbles; drain.

2 Stir beans and next 7 ingredients into beef mixture; bring to a boil. Reduce heat, and simmer, uncovered, 15 minutes, stirring occasionally.

3 Spoon soup into bowls; top with desired toppings.

Artichoke-Shrimp Bisque

8 servings

2 (10¾-ounce) cans cream of shrimp soup, undiluted

3 cups milk

½ (16-ounce) loaf mild Mexican-style process cheese spread, cubed

1 (14-ounce) can artichoke hearts, drained and chopped

¼ teaspoon seasoned salt

¼ teaspoon ground white pepper

½ teaspoon Beau Monde seasoning (optional)*

1 (5-ounce) package frozen cooked small shrimp

* If you can't find Beau Monde seasoning, substitute the same amount of seasoning salt.

1 Combine first 7 ingredients in a Dutch oven; cook over low heat until cheese melts and mixture is hot, stirring often.

2 Add shrimp; cook 1 minute or until thoroughly heated, stirring often. Spoon bisque into serving bowls.

❝No one will know how easy it is to make this rich soup! I've pumped up canned soup—so everyone will agree you cook like a professional chef!❞

Seafood Gumbo

6 servings

1½ pounds unpeeled fresh shrimp

1 (16-ounce) package smoked
  sausage, cut into ½" slices
1 clove garlic, minced

1 (16-ounce) package frozen
  vegetable gumbo mixture
1 (14½-ounce) can Cajun-style stewed
  tomatoes, undrained
1 (14½-ounce) can chicken broth

1 (6-ounce) can premium lump
  crabmeat, undrained
¼ teaspoon salt
¼ teaspoon pepper
1 tablespoon gumbo filé (optional)
Hot cooked rice

1 Peel shrimp, and devein, if desired. Set aside.

2 Cook sausage in a Dutch oven over medium-high heat, stirring constantly, until browned. Reduce heat, and add garlic; cook, stirring constantly, 1 minute.

3 Stir in frozen vegetable gumbo mixture, tomatoes, and chicken broth; bring to a boil. Reduce heat, and simmer, uncovered, 5 minutes.

4 Add shrimp, and cook 3 minutes or until shrimp turn pink. Remove from heat; stir in crabmeat, salt, pepper, and, if desired, gumbo filé. Serve gumbo over rice.

Filé Facts
Filé powder (ground dried sassafras leaves) is a mainstay in Creole cooking. Used to thicken and flavor gumbos and other Creole dishes, it also adds a little kick. Add filé at the end of cooking because heat can make it become stringy.

Camp Stew

6 servings

1 medium onion, chopped

2 (15-ounce) cans sliced potatoes, drained

2 (14.5-ounce) cans diced tomatoes, undrained

1 (15-ounce) can cream-style corn

1 (10-ounce) can roasted barbecue beef

1 (10-ounce) can roasted barbecue pork

1 (10-ounce) can white chicken, drained

¼ cup soy sauce

2 tablespoons Worcestershire sauce

1 teaspoon pepper

1 teaspoon hot pepper sauce

1 Stir together all ingredients in a large Dutch oven; bring to a boil. Reduce heat, partially cover, and simmer 20 to 30 minutes, stirring often.

What could be easier than opening cans for a taste-like-it-simmered-all-day stew? Southerners will recognize this as a shortcut version of Brunswick stew. I like to serve this with a slice of my quick Easy Beer Bread (page 145).

Ham and Bean Pot

8 servings

2 tablespoons butter
1 large onion, chopped
1 large green bell pepper, chopped

2 cups coarsely chopped cooked ham
2 (16-ounce) cans navy beans
1 (15.5-ounce) can field peas with
   jalapeño peppers or regular
   black-eyed peas
1 (15-ounce) can chunky bean and
   ham soup
1 (11½-ounce) can condensed bean
   and bacon soup, undiluted
2¾ cups water

1 Melt butter in a Dutch oven; add onion and bell pepper, and cook, stirring constantly, until tender.

2 Stir in ham and remaining ingredients; bring to a boil. Reduce heat, partially cover, and simmer 30 minutes or to desired consistency, stirring occasionally.

" I love to get cooked-all-day flavor without a lot of fuss—and this recipe's got it! If you want a little kick, stir in some salsa or black pepper. If you can't find the can sizes or the beans called for here, use something close; this is an accommodating recipe. "

White Chili

8 to 10 servings

2 medium onions, chopped
1 tablespoon olive oil

2 (4.5-ounce) cans chopped green chiles, undrained
4 cloves garlic, minced
2 teaspoons ground cumin
1½ teaspoons dried oregano
Dash of ground red pepper

6 cups chicken broth
5 cups chopped cooked chicken breast
3 (15.8-ounce) cans Great Northern beans, drained
Salt and pepper to taste
3 cups (12 ounces) shredded Monterey Jack cheese with peppers, divided

Toppings: sour cream, salsa, chopped fresh parsley or cilantro

1 Cook onions in oil in a Dutch oven over medium-high heat, stirring constantly, until tender.

2 Add green chiles and next 4 ingredients; cook, stirring constantly, 2 minutes.

3 Add chicken broth, chicken, beans, and salt and pepper to taste. Bring to a boil; reduce heat, and simmer, uncovered, 10 minutes, stirring often. Stir in 2 cups cheese; cook until cheese melts.

4 To serve, ladle chili into individual soup bowls. Top evenly with remaining 1 cup cheese and the desired toppings.

Orange-Rice Salad

4 servings

4¼ cups water
⅔ cup uncooked wild rice
1⅓ cups uncooked brown rice

½ cup chopped pecans, toasted
6 green onions, chopped
¼ cup minced fresh parsley
2 tablespoons butter
½ teaspoon salt
½ teaspoon pepper
Orange Vinaigrette

1 Bring 4¼ cups water to a boil in a saucepan; add wild rice. Reduce heat, and simmer, uncovered, 15 minutes. Stir in brown rice; cover and simmer 30 minutes or until rice is tender and water is absorbed.

2 Stir in pecans and next 5 ingredients. Toss with Orange Vinaigrette. Transfer to a bowl; cover and chill 2 hours.

Orange Vinaigrette

½ cup olive oil
¼ cup white balsamic vinegar or white wine vinegar
1 tablespoon grated orange rind
⅓ cup fresh orange juice
2 cloves garlic

Process all ingredients in a blender until smooth, stopping once to scrape down sides. Yield: 1 cup.

Quick Fix

You can substitute 2 (6-ounce) packages long-grain-and-wild rice mix for the wild and brown rices. Omit the 4¼ cups water, and prepare mix according to package directions. Proceed with Step 2.

Fusilli Fruit Salad

4 to 6 servings

2   ounces fusilli (corkscrew) pasta,
       uncooked (2⅔ cups)
1   (8-ounce) can pineapple chunks,
       undrained

1   cup cubed cantaloupe or honeydew
       melon
1   cup seedless green or red grapes

1   (8-ounce) carton peach low-fat
       yogurt
2   tablespoons sour cream

1   cup fresh strawberries, halved
Lettuce leaves

1 Cook pasta according to package directions; drain. Drain pineapple, reserving 2 tablespoons juice.

2 Combine pineapple, pasta, melon, and grapes in a large bowl. Cover and chill at least 1 hour.

3 Combine reserved pineapple juice, yogurt, and sour cream; cover yogurt dressing, and chill.

4 Toss strawberries with fruit mixture. Serve on lettuce-lined salad plates. Drizzle with yogurt dressing.

Here's a surprise—pasta in fruit salad! If you want a shortcut, buy the cantaloupe, already cut, in the produce section of your grocery store. This salad is best when the fruit and dressing are chilled separately before serving.

Apple-Spinach Salad

6 servings

1 (10-ounce) package fresh spinach, torn
2 Granny Smith apples, chopped
½ cup cashews
¼ cup golden raisins

¼ cup sugar
¼ cup apple cider vinegar
¼ cup vegetable oil
¼ teaspoon garlic salt
¼ teaspoon celery salt

1 Combine first 4 ingredients in a large bowl.

2 Combine sugar and remaining 4 ingredients in a jar; cover tightly, and shake vigorously. Pour over spinach mixture, tossing gently.

" I love how the tart, crisp apples and salty cashews contrast with the sweet-and-sour dressing that tops my salad. You can substitute pear, mandarin oranges, or strawberries for the apple, and enjoy it any time of the year! For a head start on this salad, make the dressing a day or two ahead and chill it. "

Tossed Salad with Country Buttermilk Dressing

4 servings

2   cups tightly packed torn romaine lettuce
2   cups tightly packed torn leaf lettuce
12 cherry tomatoes, halved
½   cup sliced purple onion
¼   cup chopped celery
Country Buttermilk Dressing

1 Combine first 5 ingredients in a large bowl; toss well. Toss with Country Buttermilk Dressing. Serve immediately.

Country Buttermilk Dressing

1   cup mayonnaise
1   cup buttermilk
1   tablespoon minced onion
1   tablespoon minced fresh parsley
¼   teaspoon garlic powder

Combine all ingredients, mixing well. Chill at least 2 hours. Yield: 2 cups.

Greek Salad

(pictured on back cover)
4 to 6 servings

2 medium tomatoes, cut into wedges
1 medium zucchini, cut into thin strips
1 medium cucumber, sliced
1 cup pitted ripe olives
1 medium-size purple onion, thinly
   sliced and separated into rings
¾ cup feta cheese, crumbled

1 (6-ounce) jar marinated artichoke
   hearts, undrained

¼ cup red wine vinegar
¼ teaspoon freshly ground pepper
Lettuce leaves

1 Combine first 6 ingredients in a large bowl; toss gently, and set aside.

2 Drain artichoke hearts, reserving marinade. Add artichoke hearts to tomato mixture.

3 Combine reserved marinade, vinegar and pepper; pour over tomato mixture, and toss. Cover and chill 8 hours. Drain; serve on lettuce.

66 Tangy feta cheese, ripe olives, and marinated artichokes give you a delicious break from boring salads. My secret? Marinating everything but the lettuce in the morning so that I've got a knockout salad for supper!99

Best Barbecue Coleslaw

8 to 10 servings

2   (10-ounce) packages finely
    shredded cabbage
1   carrot, peeled and shredded

½   cup sugar
½   teaspoon salt
⅛   teaspoon pepper
½   cup mayonnaise
¼   cup milk
¼   cup buttermilk
2½ tablespoons lemon juice
1½ tablespoons white vinegar

1 Combine cabbage and carrot in a large bowl.

2 Whisk together sugar and remaining 7 ingredients until blended; toss with vegetables. Cover and chill at least 2 hours.

Sizing Up Your Need

This makes a big batch of coleslaw, and leftovers will keep a couple of days in the fridge. If you don't need such a large amount, you can easily cut the recipe in half.

Confetti Corn Toss

6 to 8 servings

2   (15¼-ounce) cans whole kernel
    corn, drained
1   (15-ounce) can black beans, rinsed
    and drained
1   (14.8-ounce) can hearts of palm,
    drained and sliced
2   large tomatoes, seeded and
    chopped
½   cup chopped purple onion
⅓   cup minced fresh cilantro

¼   cup vegetable oil
3   tablespoons lime juice
1½ teaspoons chili powder
½   teaspoon ground cumin
Tortilla chips

1 Combine first 6 ingredients in a large bowl.

2 Combine oil and next 3 ingredients, stirring well; drizzle over salad, and toss gently. Cover and chill 3 hours. Serve with tortilla chips.

" I've added a few fresh ingredients to some canned vegetables for this zesty side dish that'll have all the neighbors talkin'! Cilantro, lime juice, and cumin spike my recipe with a south-of-the-border flair. It's so versatile, you can also serve it as a salad or salsa!"

Green Bean, Walnut, and Feta Salad

6 servings

¾ cup olive oil

¼ cup white wine vinegar

1 tablespoon chopped fresh dill
   (optional)

½ teaspoon minced garlic

¼ teaspoon salt

¼ teaspoon pepper

1 ½ pounds fresh green beans

1 cup coarsely chopped walnuts,
   toasted

1 small purple onion, thinly sliced

1 (4-ounce) package crumbled feta
   cheese

1 Combine first 6 ingredients; cover and chill.

2 Wash beans; trim ends, and remove strings. Cut beans into thirds, and arrange in a steamer basket over boiling water. Cover and steam 10 minutes or until beans are crisp-tender. Immediately plunge beans into cold water to stop the cooking process; drain and pat dry.

3 Combine beans, walnuts, onion slices, and cheese in a large bowl; toss well. Cover and chill.

4 Pour oil mixture over bean mixture 1 hour before serving; toss just before serving.

Toast Walnuts for Flavor

Tart feta cheese and earthy toasted walnuts go great with crisp fresh green beans. To toast the walnuts for this recipe, bake them in a shallow pan at 350° for 5 to 10 minutes or until toasted, stirring occasionally.

Tuna-Filled Tomatoes

4 servings

3 hard-cooked eggs, coarsely chopped

1 (9-ounce) can tuna, drained and flaked

¾ cup sliced celery

¼ cup sliced green onions

¼ cup sweet pickle relish

¼ to ⅓ cup mayonnaise or salad dressing

¼ teaspoon lemon pepper

⅛ teaspoon salt

3 drops of hot pepper sauce

4 medium tomatoes

Lettuce leaves
Paprika

1 Combine first 9 ingredients; cover and chill.

2 Core tomatoes. Cut each into 6 wedges, cutting to, but not through, base of tomato.

3 Arrange each tomato on a lettuce-lined plate. Spoon tuna mixture into tomatoes; sprinkle with paprika.

Tomato Tidbits

Most fresh tomatoes sold at the supermarket are firm and not yet ripe. This keeps them from bruising during shipping. Tomatoes will ripen properly if kept at room temperature. Once they're ripe, you can chill them in the refrigerator—but only for a few days; any longer and they'll begin to lose flavor.

Mexican Beef Salad

(pictured on page 106)

6 servings

2 teaspoons taco seasoning mix
2 teaspoons vegetable oil
1 pound flank steak

1 (8-ounce) carton sour cream
1 (4.5-ounce) can chopped green
chiles, undrained
1½ teaspoons taco seasoning mix

Nonstick cooking spray
6 (10") flour tortillas

6 cups shredded lettuce
1 cup chopped fresh cilantro
2 tomatoes, chopped
1 cup frozen whole kernel corn,
thawed
¾ cup drained canned dark red kidney
beans
Toppings: grated cheese, pickled
jalapeño slices, chopped green
onions, salsa (optional)

1 Combine 2 teaspoons taco seasoning mix and oil; rub evenly over both sides of steak. Cover; chill 30 minutes.

2 Combine sour cream, chiles, and 1½ teaspoons taco seasoning mix in a small bowl. Cover and chill.

3 Preheat the oven to Broil. Coat a medium-size microwave-safe bowl with nonstick cooking spray. Press 1 tortilla gently into bowl. Microwave at HIGH setting 1½ minutes. Remove from bowl, and set aside. Repeat procedure with remaining tortillas.

4 Place steak on a rack of a broiler pan coated with nonstick cooking spray. Broil 5½" from heat (with electric oven door partially opened), 8 minutes on each side or to desired degree of doneness. Cut steak in half lengthwise. Slice each half diagonally across grain into thin strips.

5 Combine lettuce and cilantro; place lettuce mixture evenly into tortilla bowls. Top with tomatoes, corn, beans, and steak. Spoon sour cream mixture evenly over each serving. Serve with desired toppings.

BLT Chicken Salad

4 servings

½ cup mayonnaise
¼ cup barbecue sauce
2 tablespoons grated onion
1 tablespoon lemon juice
½ teaspoon pepper

2 large tomatoes, chopped

8 cups torn leaf lettuce or iceberg
    lettuce
2 hard-cooked eggs, sliced
3 cups chopped cooked chicken

10 slices bacon, cooked and crumbled

1 Combine first 5 ingredients in a small bowl; stir well. Cover dressing, and chill thoroughly.

2 Press chopped tomato between several layers of paper towels to remove excess moisture.

3 Arrange lettuce on individual salad plates; top each serving with egg slices, tomatoes, and chicken.

4 Spoon dressing over salads; sprinkle with crumbled bacon. Serve salad immediately.

BLTs don't mean just sandwiches anymore! This favorite trio brings a twist to chicken salad. And I think you'll agree my homemade salad dressing takes it over the top!

Breadshoppe Bounty

"From savory biscuits to sweet pastries, my speedy breads will delight you with their made-from-scratch flavor!!"

Cheddar 'n' Chive Drop Biscuits

16 biscuits

3   cups biscuit mix
1   cup (4 ounces) finely shredded
      sharp Cheddar cheese
1   tablespoon chopped fresh chives or
      dried chives
½   teaspoon garlic powder

1   cup milk
½   cup sour cream

3   tablespoons butter, melted

1 Preheat the oven to 425°. Combine first 4 ingredients in a large bowl; stir well. Make a well in center of mixture.

2 Combine milk and sour cream in a bowl; add to dry ingredients, stirring just until dry ingredients are moistened.

3 Drop by ¼ cupfuls onto a lightly greased baking sheet; brush with butter. Bake at 425° for 8 to 10 minutes or until golden.

Throw away your rolling pin and forget the floury mess!! 'Drop' biscuits get their name from their method. Instead of rolling and cutting them like traditional biscuits, you simply 'drop' the dough straight from a spoon or measuring cup onto a baking sheet.

Dill Biscuits

10 servings

¼ cup butter, melted
1 tablespoon dried dillweed
3 tablespoons finely chopped onion

1 (12-ounce) can refrigerated
 buttermilk biscuits

1 Preheat the oven to 400°. Combine first 3 ingredients in a bowl.

2 Cut biscuits in half. Dip each biscuit piece in butter mixture; arrange biscuits in a single layer in an ungreased 8"-square pan.

3 Bake at 400° for 12 to 14 minutes. Serve immediately.

Try These Twists!

Easy Sweet Twists: Omit dillweed and onion. Combine ½ cup sugar and 1 teaspoon ground cinnamon; set aside. Instead of cutting biscuits in half, roll each into a 9" rope. Dip in melted butter, and coat with sugar mixture. Twist several times, and place on a lightly greased baking sheet. Bake at 400° for 10 to 12 minutes. Makes 10 twists.

Cheesy Twists: Substitute ½ cup grated Parmesan cheese and ½ teaspoon Dijon mustard for dillweed and onion, and reduce melted butter to 3 tablespoons. Instead of cutting biscuits in half, roll each biscuit into a 2" x 5" rectangle; spread about 2 teaspoons cheese mixture over rectangle, and, using a pizza cutter, cut in half lengthwise. Twist each half 2 or 3 times, and place on a lightly greased baking sheet. Bake at 400° for 8 to 10 minutes or until golden. Makes 20 twists.

Savory Sausage-Swiss Muffins

1 dozen

½   pound mild or spicy ground pork
     sausage

1¾   cups biscuit mix
½   cup (2 ounces) shredded Swiss
     cheese
¾   teaspoon ground sage
¼   teaspoon dried thyme

1   large egg, lightly beaten
½   cup milk

1 Preheat the oven to 375°. Brown sausage in a skillet over medium heat, stirring until it crumbles. Drain well.

2 Combine sausage, biscuit mix, and next 3 ingredients in a bowl; make a well in center of mixture.

3 Combine egg and milk; add to dry ingredients, stirring just until dry ingredients are moistened. Spoon batter into greased muffin pans, filling two-thirds full.

4 Bake at 375° for 22 minutes or until golden. Serve warm. Store leftovers in refrigerator.

A Quick Morning Meal

Swiss cheese and sausage make these savory muffins perfect breakfast fare. You can even make them ahead to keep in the fridge until you're ready for them. To reheat, microwave 1 muffin at HIGH setting 20 to 30 seconds or until hot. Just add coffee and fresh fruit, and you'll have a filling breakfast ready in a flash!

Pumpkin-Raisin Muffins

3 dozen

2 (15.4-ounce) packages nut bread mix
1 ¼ cups golden raisins

2 large eggs, lightly beaten
1 (30-ounce) can pumpkin pie filling

1 Preheat the oven to 400°. Combine bread mix and raisins in a large bowl; make a well in center of mixture.

2 Combine eggs and pie filling; add to dry ingredients, stirring just until dry ingredients are moistened. Place paper baking cups in muffin pans; spoon batter into cups, filling two-thirds full.

3 Bake at 400° for 15 to 20 minutes. Remove from pans immediately, and cool on wire racks.

I shave time from making traditional pumpkin bread by using a boxed bread mix and a can of pumpkin pie filling. What could be easier? I just stir together four simple ingredients, pour into muffin pans, and bake. It's easy as 1-2-3!!

Mexican Hush Puppies

2 dozen

¾ cup self-rising cornmeal
½ cup self-rising flour
⅛ teaspoon ground red pepper
1 cup (4 ounces) shredded Monterey
    Jack cheese
1 (4.5-ounce) can chopped green
    chiles, drained
1 tablespoon minced onion

1 large egg, lightly beaten
½ cup milk

Vegetable oil

1 Stir together first 6 ingredients in a large bowl; make a well in center of mixture.

2 Combine egg and milk; add to dry ingredients, stirring just until dry ingredients are moistened.

3 Pour oil to depth of 2" into a Dutch oven; heat to 375°. Drop batter by rounded tablespoonfuls into oil; fry 2 to 3 minutes or until hush puppies are golden, turning once. Drain on paper towels.

" Don't wait for a fish fry to make my hush puppies! Monterey Jack cheese and green chiles spice up these crispy hot bites, making them irresistible! To make sure the hush puppies are round, I use a small (1") ice cream scoop to drop the batter into the hot oil. "

Muffin Tin Popovers

1 dozen

1 cup all-purpose flour
¼ teaspoon salt
1 cup milk
2 large eggs, lightly beaten

1 Preheat the oven to 425°. Combine all ingredients; beat at low speed of an electric beater just until smooth.

2 Place a well-greased muffin pan in a 425° oven for 3 minutes or until a drop of water sizzles when dropped in it. Remove pan from oven; spoon batter into cups, filling two-thirds full.

3 Bake at 425° for 15 minutes. Reduce heat to 350°, and bake 18 to 20 minutes. Turn oven off. Pierce each popover with the tip of a sharp knife to let steam escape. Keep popovers in hot oven 5 more minutes to crisp. Serve hot.

Popover Magic

You don't need a fancy popover pan for these popovers! The batter bakes up into crispy rolls in a regular muffin pan. The leavening power in eggs causes the popovers to rise high above their pans once in the oven. Be sure to resist the temptation to open the oven door as they bake!

Parsley-Garlic Rolls

(pictured on page 107)

1 dozen

2   tablespoons chopped fresh parsley
3   tablespoons butter, melted
2   cloves garlic, pressed

1   (16-ounce) loaf frozen bread
     dough, thawed

Garnish: fresh parsley sprigs

1 Combine first 3 ingredients; set mixture aside.

2 Roll bread dough into a 12" square; spread parsley mixture over dough, leaving a ½" border on top and bottom edges. Roll dough tightly, jellyroll fashion, starting at bottom edge. Press top edge of dough into roll to seal edge. Cut roll of dough into 1"-wide slices. Place slices, cut sides down, in lightly greased muffin pans.

3 Cover and let rise in a warm place (85°), free from drafts, 1 hour or until doubled in bulk. Preheat the oven to 400°.

4 Bake at 400° for 9 to 11 minutes or until golden. Remove from pans, and serve immediately. Garnish, if desired.

Buttery Italian Breadsticks

6 servings

1	(11-ounce) can refrigerated breadstick dough
¼	cup butter, melted
1½	teaspoons garlic powder
2	teaspoons dried Italian seasoning

¾ cup (3 ounces) shredded mozzarella cheese
Spaghetti sauce (optional)

1 Preheat the oven to 350°. Cut each breadstick in half crosswise; place on a large baking sheet. Brush generously with butter. Sprinkle with garlic powder and Italian seasoning.

2 Bake at 350° for 10 to 13 minutes; sprinkle with cheese, and bake 3 to 5 more minutes or until cheese melts and breadsticks are golden. Serve with spaghetti sauce for dipping, if desired.

A Spicy Variation

Buttery Southwestern Breadsticks: Substitute 1 teaspoon chili powder and ½ teaspoon ground cumin for Italian seasoning, and shredded Monterey Jack cheese for mozzarella cheese. Proceed with Step 1. Serve with Ranch-style dressing for dipping, if desired.

Greek Bread

1 loaf

1 (8-ounce) package cream cheese, softened
2 tablespoons mayonnaise
2 teaspoons Greek seasoning
1 (16-ounce) loaf unsliced French bread

1 (4-ounce) package crumbled tomato-basil or plain feta cheese
1 (2¼-ounce) can sliced ripe olives, drained
½ cup drained, chopped peperoncini peppers

1 Preheat the oven to 375°. Combine first 3 ingredients, stirring until smooth. Slice bread loaf in half horizontally. Spread cream cheese mixture on cut sides of bread.

2 Sprinkle feta cheese, olives, and peppers over cream cheese mixture. Place bread on an ungreased baking sheet. Bake at 375° for 15 minutes or until thoroughly heated.

" One bite of this cheesy bread will have you craving more, more, more! And when I say cheesy, I mean it—cream cheese and feta take this anytime bread over the top!"

Fast Italian Flat Bread

10 servings

2	green onions, thinly sliced
⅓	cup grated Parmesan cheese
⅓	cup mayonnaise
1	clove garlic, minced, or ⅛ teaspoon garlic powder
¼	teaspoon dried basil
¼	teaspoon dried oregano
1	(12-ounce) can refrigerated flaky biscuits

1 Preheat the oven to 400°. Combine first 6 ingredients in a small bowl; stir well.

2 Press each biscuit into a 4" circle on an ungreased baking sheet. Spread about 1 tablespoon cheese mixture evenly on circles, leaving a ¼" border.

3 Bake at 400° for 9 to 11 minutes or until golden. Serve warm.

A Pizzalike Treat

Traditionally, flat bread is thin and crisp like a cracker. Here, flattened canned biscuits serve as a bread base that's similar to a pizza crust. No matter the name, you're sure to call it *"OOH IT'S SO GOOD!!"*

Broccoli Cornbread

12 squares

1 (10-ounce) package frozen chopped
    broccoli, thawed

1 (8½-ounce) package corn
    muffin mix
4 large eggs, lightly beaten
¾ cup small-curd cottage cheese
½ cup butter or margarine, melted
⅓ cup chopped onion
1 teaspoon salt

1 Preheat the oven to 400°. Drain broccoli well, pressing between paper towels.

2 Combine corn muffin mix and remaining 5 ingredients; stir well. Stir in broccoli. Pour into a greased 9" x 13" baking dish.

3 Bake at 400° for 20 to 25 minutes or until golden. Let cool slightly, and cut into squares.

Easy Beer Bread

1 loaf

3   cups self-rising flour
3   tablespoons sugar
1   (12-ounce) can beer (at room
       temperature)

2   to 3 tablespoons butter, melted

1 Preheat the oven to 350°. Combine flour and sugar in a large bowl. Gradually add beer, stirring just until dry ingredients are moistened.

2 Spoon batter into a greased and floured 4½" x 8½" loafpan. Bake at 350° for 55 to 60 minutes or until a toothpick inserted in center comes out clean.

3 Brush top with butter. Cool loaf in pan 10 minutes; remove from pan, and cool completely on a wire rack. Slice with a serrated knife.

When I say easy, I'm not kidding! Four ingredients (including my secret ingredient, beer) rise to the occasion in this loaf. Self-rising flour has baking powder and salt added to it. It makes quick work of this already quick bread.

Nutty Wheat Loaf

1 loaf

1¼ cups all-purpose flour
1 cup whole wheat flour
2 teaspoons baking powder
¾ teaspoon salt
1 cup packed dark brown sugar
½ cup coarsely chopped walnuts
½ cup wheat germ
1 teaspoon ground cinnamon
½ teaspoon ground nutmeg

2 large eggs, lightly beaten
1¼ cups milk
½ cup butter, melted

1 Preheat the oven to 350°. Combine first 9 ingredients in a large mixing bowl; stir well.

2 Combine eggs, milk, and butter; add to dry ingredients, stirring just until dry ingredients are moistened. Spoon batter into a greased and floured 4½" x 8½" loafpan.

3 Bake at 350° for 55 to 60 minutes or until a toothpick inserted in center comes out clean. Cool loaf in pan on a wire rack.

A Fresh Test
Baking powder is what makes quick breads quick—it eliminates the need for bread to rise. But for it to work, baking powder needs to be fresh. Most brands have an expiration date on the can. If there isn't a date, here's a quick test for freshness: Add a teaspoon of baking powder to a half cup of hot water. The mixture should foam vigorously. If it doesn't, throw away the can!!

Eggnog Tea Bread

4 loaves

1   (16-ounce) package pound cake mix
¾   cup refrigerated eggnog
½   teaspoon ground nutmeg
2   large eggs

1   cup sifted powdered sugar
2   tablespoons refrigerated eggnog

1 Preheat the oven to 350°. Combine first 4 ingredients in a large mixing bowl; beat at medium speed of an electric beater 3 minutes.

2 Pour batter into 4 greased 3" x 6" loafpans. Bake at 350° for 30 minutes or until a toothpick inserted in center comes out clean. Remove from pans; cool on wire racks.

3 Combine powdered sugar and 2 tablespoons eggnog, stirring well; drizzle over bread. Store in refrigerator.

Loafin' Around

These little loaves are great for gift giving, especially around the holidays. But if you just want to indulge yourself, it's easy to make 1 large loaf: Just pour the batter into a greased 5" x 9" loafpan. Bake at 350° for 48 to 50 minutes or until a toothpick inserted in center comes out clean.

Cinnamon-Raisin Swirl Bread

1 loaf

1   (17.4-ounce) can refrigerated
    home-style loaf bread
2   tablespoons butter, melted
3   tablespoons sugar
2   teaspoons ground cinnamon
¼   cup raisins, chopped

½   cup sifted powdered sugar
1   tablespoon milk
⅛   teaspoon vanilla extract

If you thought you could get this bread only from the bakery, you've got to try MY recipe! Convenient canned bread dough lays the foundation for butter, cinnamon, and raisins, all wrapped up in one delicious loaf!

1 Carefully unroll loaf bread dough into a 7" x 18" rectangle. Brush dough with melted butter. Combine sugar and cinnamon; sprinkle sugar mixture and raisins over melted butter. Roll up dough, starting at short side, and pinch ends to seal.

2 Place dough, seam side down, in a well-greased 4½" x 8½" loafpan. Let stand in a warm place (85°), free from drafts, 30 minutes. Preheat the oven to 350°.

3 Bake loaf at 350° for 35 minutes or until golden. Remove loaf from pan immediately; let cool on a wire rack at least 1 hour.

4 Combine powdered sugar, milk, and vanilla, stirring until smooth. Drizzle over loaf. To serve, slice loaf with a serrated knife. Store in refrigerator.

Chocolate Chip Scones

8 scones

2½ cups all-purpose flour
2   teaspoons baking powder
½   teaspoon salt
½   cup sugar
⅓   cup butter

1¼ cups whipping cream
1   cup (6 ounces) semisweet
      chocolate chips

1 Preheat the oven to 400°. Combine first 4 ingredients; cut in butter with pastry blender or 2 knives until crumbly.

2 Reserve 1 tablespoon cream; add remaining cream and chocolate chips to dry ingredients, stirring just until dry ingredients are moistened.

3 Turn dough out onto a lightly floured surface; knead 5 or 6 times. Shape into an 8" circle on a lightly greased baking sheet. Cut circle into 8 wedges (do not separate). Prick wedges with a fork 3 or 4 times, and brush with reserved 1 tablespoon whipping cream.

4 Bake at 400° for 25 minutes or until lightly browned. Serve warm with whipped cream, if desired.

And for Fruit Lovers . . .

Raisin Scones: Substitute ¾ cup raisins for the chocolate chips, and add ¼ teaspoon cinnamon with dry ingredients.

Cranberry Scones: Substitute ¾ cup dried sweetened cranberries or fresh or frozen cranberries, chopped, for chocolate. Add ¼ teaspoon cinnamon to flour mixture.

Nutty Crescent Twists

8 twists

2   (8-ounce) cans refrigerated
    crescent rolls
6   tablespoons butter, melted and
    divided

½   cup chopped pecans or walnuts
¼   cup sugar
1   teaspoon ground cinnamon
⅛   teaspoon ground nutmeg

½   cup sifted powdered sugar
2   tablespoons maple syrup

1 Preheat the oven to 375°. Unroll crescent rolls, and separate each can into 4 rectangles, pressing perforations to seal. Brush evenly with 4 tablespoons melted butter.

2 Stir together pecans and next 3 ingredients; sprinkle 1 tablespoon mixture on each rectangle, pressing in gently.

3 Roll up, starting at a long side, and twist. Cut 6 shallow (½" long) diagonal slits in each roll. Shape rolls into rings, pressing ends together; place on a lightly greased baking sheet.

4 Brush rings with remaining 2 tablespoons butter. Bake at 375° for 12 minutes or until golden.

5 Stir together powdered sugar and maple syrup until glaze is smooth; drizzle over warm twists.

Praline French Toast

8 servings

8   large eggs, lightly beaten
1½   cups half-and-half
1   tablespoon brown sugar
2   teaspoons vanilla extract
8   (1"-thick) slices French bread

½   cup butter
¾   cup packed brown sugar
½   cup maple syrup
1   (2-ounce) package chopped
       pecans (¾ cup)

1 Combine first 4 ingredients in a large bowl, stirring with a wire whisk until blended. Pour 1 cup egg mixture into a greased 9" x 13" baking dish. Place bread in dish; pour remaining egg mixture over bread. Cover and chill 8 hours.

2 Preheat the oven to 350°. Combine butter, brown sugar, maple syrup, and pecans in a microwave-safe bowl. Cover with plastic wrap, and microwave at HIGH setting 30 seconds. Pour over bread.

3 Bake, uncovered, at 350° for 30 minutes or until set and golden.

" My version of French toast is like having dessert for breakfast! A rich brown sugar glaze with crunchy pecans tops off buttery bread for a breakfast that'll have everybody singing, 'OOH IT'S SO GOOD!!'"

Cream Cheese Danish

20 squares

2   (8-ounce) cans refrigerated
     crescent rolls
1   large egg, separated
2   (8-ounce) packages cream cheese,
     softened
1   cup sugar
1   teaspoon lemon juice
1   teaspoon vanilla extract

¾   cup chopped pecans

Sifted powdered sugar

1 Preheat the oven to 375°. Unroll 1 can of rolls; press into a lightly greased 9" x 13" pan. Beat egg yolk, cream cheese, and next 3 ingredients at medium speed of an electric beater until blended; spread over dough in pan.

2 Unroll remaining can of crescent rolls on a sheet of wax paper; press into a 9" x 13" rectangle. Place over cream cheese mixture. Whisk egg white; brush over dough. Sprinkle with pecans.

3 Bake at 375° for 25 minutes. Sprinkle with powdered sugar, and cool in pan on a wire rack. Cut into squares.

❝ Tired of boxed cereal or drive-thru biscuits for breakfast? Wrap up one of my Danish squares and take it with you!❞

Sweet Inspiration

“You'll hear nothing but oohs and aahs when you whip up these delectable cakes, pies, and other sensational sweets!!”

Lemon-Poppy Seed Cake
9 servings

1⅔ cups all-purpose flour
1 teaspoon baking soda
¼ teaspoon salt
¾ cup sugar
2 teaspoons poppy seeds

1 large egg, lightly beaten
¾ cup milk
1 teaspoon grated lemon rind
3 tablespoons fresh lemon juice
3 tablespoons butter, melted

⅓ cup frozen lemonade concentrate, thawed and undiluted
1 tablespoon powdered sugar

1 Preheat the oven to 375°. Combine first 5 ingredients in a large bowl; make a well in center of mixture.

2 Combine egg and next 4 ingredients; add to dry ingredients, stirring just until moistened. Spoon batter into a greased and floured 8"-square pan.

3 Bake at 375° for 23 to 25 minutes or until a wooden toothpick inserted in center comes out clean. Cool in pan on a wire rack 10 minutes.

4 Combine lemonade concentrate and powdered sugar. Spoon over warm cake.

Vary It a Little!
Lemon-Poppy Seed Loaves: Spoon batter into 3 (3½" x 6") disposable aluminum loafpans coated with nonstick cooking spray. Bake at 375° for 20 to 22 minutes or until a wooden toothpick inserted in center comes out clean. Cool in pans on a wire rack 5 minutes. Proceed with Step 4. Makes 3 loaves.

Lemon-Poppy Seed Mini-Muffins: Spoon batter into muffin pans, filling two-thirds full. Bake at 350° for 18 minutes. Remove from pans immediately, and let cool on wire racks. Proceed with Step 4. Makes 1 dozen.

Cherry Fudge Cake

12 to 15 servings

1 (18.25-ounce) package devil's food
    cake mix with pudding
1 (21-ounce) can cherry pie filling
2 large eggs
1 teaspoon almond or vanilla extract

1 cup sugar
⅓ cup butter or margarine
⅓ cup milk

1 cup (6 ounces) semisweet chocolate
    chips

1 Preheat the oven to 350°. Combine first 4 ingredients in a bowl until blended. Pour into a greased and floured 9" x 13" pan.

2 Bake at 350° for 30 minutes or until a wooden toothpick inserted in center of cake comes out clean. Cool in pan on a wire rack.

3 Combine sugar, butter, and milk in a small saucepan. Bring to a boil, stirring constantly; reduce heat, and simmer, stirring constantly, 1 minute.

4 Remove from heat; stir in chocolate chips until blended. Pour over cooled cake, and let stand until set.

Coconut Layer Cake

1 (3-layer) cake

3   large eggs
1   (8-ounce) carton sour cream
¾   cup vegetable oil
¾   cup cream of coconut
½   teaspoon vanilla extract
1   (18.25-ounce) package white cake
      mix with pudding

Coconut-Cream Cheese Frosting

1 Preheat the oven to 325°. Grease and flour 3 (8") round cakepans. Set aside.

2 Beat eggs at high speed of an electric beater 2 minutes. Add sour cream and next 3 ingredients, beating well after each addition. Add cake mix; beat at low speed until blended. Beat at high speed 2 minutes. Pour batter evenly into prepared pans.

3 Bake at 325° for 25 to 27 minutes or until a wooden toothpick inserted in center comes out clean. Cool in pans on wire racks 10 minutes; remove from pans, and let cool completely on wire racks.

4 Spread Coconut-Cream Cheese Frosting between layers and on top and sides of cake. Sprinkle with ½ cup coconut left over from frosting. Store in an airtight container in refrigerator.

Coconut-Cream Cheese Frosting

1   (8-ounce) package cream cheese,
      softened
½   cup butter, softened
1   teaspoon vanilla extract
1   (16-ounce) package powdered
      sugar, sifted
1   (7-ounce) can flaked coconut,
      divided

While cake layers are baking, beat cream cheese and butter at medium speed of an electric beater until creamy; add vanilla, beating well. Gradually add sugar, beating until smooth. Reserve ½ cup coconut for Step 4 of recipe above; stir remaining coconut into frosting. Yield: 4 cups.

Mocha Brownie Cake

(pictured on page 4)

1 (2-layer) cake

1 (23.7-ounce) package double fudge
    brownie mix
⅓ cup water
¼ cup vegetable oil
3 large eggs, lightly beaten
½ cup chopped pecans

1½ cups heavy whipping cream
1 tablespoon instant coffee granules
¼ cup sifted powdered sugar
Garnish: chocolate shavings

1 Preheat the oven to 350°. Coat
2 (8") cakepans with nonstick cooking
spray; line pans with wax paper, and
coat with cooking spray. Set aside.

2 Combine first 4 ingredients; stir in
pecans. Spread batter evenly into
prepared pans. Bake at 350° for 25 minutes. Let cool in pans on wire racks 5
minutes; invert onto wire racks. Carefully
remove wax paper; let cake layers cool
completely on wire racks.

3 Combine whipping cream and coffee
granules. Beat at medium speed of
an electric beater until foamy; gradually
add powdered sugar, beating until stiff
peaks form. Spread whipped cream
mixture between layers and on top and
sides of cake. Cover and chill 1 to 2
hours. Garnish, if desired.

*" I've found that chilling
or freezing the mixing bowls
and beaters about 15 minutes
before beating the whipping cream
helps give the frosting more volume!
Once I've frosted the cake, I chill it
to give the frosting time to set and to
make the cake easier to slice and
serve. "*

Neapolitan Cake

1 (10") cake

1   (10") round angel food
     cake (store-bought)

½   gallon Neapolitan ice cream,
     softened

1   (2.6-ounce) package whipped
     topping mix

Garnish: whole strawberries

1 Using a serrated knife, cut cake horizontally into 4 equal layers. Place bottom cake layer on a serving plate.

2 Slice ice cream into thirds according to flavors. Spread top of bottom cake layer with chocolate ice cream. Top with second cake layer; spread with vanilla ice cream. Top with third cake layer; spread with strawberry ice cream. Top with remaining cake layer. Cover and freeze 1 hour.

3 Prepare both envelopes of whipped topping mix according to package directions.

4 Remove cake from freezer, and spread top and sides with whipped topping. Cover loosely; freeze until firm.

5 Let stand at room temperature 10 minutes before serving. Garnish, if desired.

> *My secret to warm-weather entertaining? No cooking—no kidding! This three-ingredient cake helps me keep my cool whether I've got guests or just feel like whipping up an OOH-SO-EASY dessert!*

Easy Petits Fours

20 petits fours

2   (10.75-ounce) loaves pound cake

8   (2-ounce) vanilla-flavored almond
       bark candy coating squares
½   cup whipping cream
2   colors of liquid food color

1   (4¼-ounce) tube white decorator
       frosting

1 Trim ¼" off top and sides of each cake. Cut each cake into 5 (1½"-thick) slices; cut each slice into 2 (1½"-thick) squares.

2 Combine candy coating and whipping cream in a microwave-safe bowl; cover with plastic wrap, and fold back a small corner of wrap to vent. Microwave at MEDIUM setting (50% power) 4 minutes, stirring once. Divide coating into 2 portions; stir 1 drop of desired food color into each portion of coating.

3 Spear the bottom of each cake square with a fork, and dip into desired colored coating. Place upright on a wire rack until frosting is set. Repeat with remaining cake squares and coating, microwaving coating at MEDIUM setting (50% power) 30 seconds if coating starts to firm up. Repeat dipping procedure for a thicker coating, if desired.

4 Using decorator frosting and star tip, pipe desired designs on top of petits fours.

Easy 3-Step Blueberry-Swirl Cheesecake

8 servings

2   (8-ounce) packages cream cheese,
       softened
½   cup sugar
2   large eggs
¼   teaspoon vanilla extract

1   (9-inch) graham cracker crust
1   (21-ounce) can blueberry pie filling,
       divided

1 Preheat the oven to 350°. Beat cream cheese at medium speed of an electric beater until creamy; gradually add sugar, beating well. Add eggs, one at a time, beating after each addition. Stir in vanilla.

2 Pour cream cheese mixture into graham cracker crust; spoon ⅔ cup blueberry pie filling over cream cheese mixture. Swirl gently with a knife to create a marbled effect. Cover remaining pie filling, and store in refrigerator.

3 Bake cheesecake at 350° for 40 minutes or until center is set. Let cool completely in pan on a wire rack. Cover and chill 8 hours. Spread reserved pie filling over cheesecake before serving.

" Making a cheesecake just doesn't get any easier than with my three-step version. A ready-made crust and canned pie filling take care of most of the fuss. "

Snappy Turtle Cheesecake

8 servings

1   (23.5-ounce) frozen French
      cheesecake

½   cup caramel topping
¾   cup lightly salted cashew halves,
      coarsely chopped
⅓   (7.25-ounce) bottle chocolate fudge
      shell topping

1 Remove cheesecake from package, and place on a serving plate.

2 Spoon caramel topping evenly over top of cheesecake; sprinkle with cashews. Shake shell topping 20 seconds before using. Drizzle shell topping over cashews, allowing it to drip down sides of cake.

3 Chill cheesecake until shell topping hardens.

Dessert in a Snap!
Why slave for hours to make cheesecake from scratch when you can make this delicious, sinful recipe in a matter of minutes? Start with a store-bought cheesecake, and top with cashews, caramel topping, and fudge topping. Dessert's on the table in no time!

Brownie-Mint Pie

1 (9") pie

1   (4.6-ounce) package chocolate
       mints

1 Preheat the oven to 350°. Chop chocolate mints, and set aside 3 tablespoons.

1   (15.8-ounce) package brownie mix
1   unbaked 9" deep-dish frozen
       pastry shell

2 Prepare brownie mix according to package directions, stirring remaining chopped mints into brownie batter. Pour into pastry shell.

Vanilla ice cream
Hot fudge topping, warmed

3 Bake at 350° for 45 minutes or until done; cool slightly. Serve topped with ice cream, hot fudge topping, and reserved 3 tablespoons chopped chocolate mints.

" Hot fudge topping over vanilla ice cream and my gooey brownie pie sends me over the edge! It's a chocolate lover's dream, and 'OOH IT'S SO GOOD!!' "

Peanut Butter Pie

1 (9") pie

½ (8-ounce) package cream cheese, softened
1 cup sifted powdered sugar

½ cup milk
⅓ cup creamy peanut butter
1 (8-ounce) container frozen whipped topping, thawed

1 (9-inch) graham cracker crust
Hot fudge topping, warmed

1 Beat cream cheese at high speed of an electric beater until creamy; gradually add sugar, beating well.

2 Add milk and peanut butter; beat until smooth. Gently fold in whipped topping.

3 Spoon mixture into crust; cover and freeze until firm. Serve with hot fudge topping.

A Freezer Delight!
This cool and creamy pie will be a favorite with your whole gang because of its rich peanut butter flavor. And you'll love it, too, because it's extra, extra simple and doesn't even need to bake! Make it ahead to have on hand for unexpected guests.

Florida Frost Pie

1 (9") pie

1½ cups gingersnap crumbs
¼   cup butter, melted
2   tablespoons sugar

½   gallon orange sherbet, softened
3   tablespoons fresh lemon juice
2   teaspoons grated orange rind

1 Preheat the oven to 375°. Combine first 3 ingredients. Firmly press crumb mixture evenly in bottom and up sides of a 9" pie plate.

2 Bake at 375° for 6 to 8 minutes or until edges are browned. Cool completely on a wire rack.

3 Combine orange sherbet, lemon juice, and 1½ teaspoons orange rind in a large bowl; stir well. Spoon sherbet mixture into prepared crust, mounding and swirling with a small spatula. Sprinkle with remaining ½ teaspoon orange rind. Freeze pie until firm.

Sure-Bet Sherbets

A slice of this frosty pie inspired by the Sunshine State will surely cool things down when it's hot outside! Any flavor of sherbet–lime, raspberry, whichever's your favorite–works well in this pie. Just omit the orange rind if you use a flavor other than orange.

Coffee Ice Cream Pie

1 (10") pie

½ cup butter, melted
½ cup chopped nuts
2 tablespoons all-purpose flour
1 (7-ounce) can flaked coconut

½ gallon coffee ice cream, softened

1 cup whipping cream
¼ cup sifted powdered sugar
Chocolate curls (optional)

½ cup Kahlúa or other coffee-flavored
     liqueur (optional)

1 Preheat the oven to 375°. Combine first 4 ingredients; press mixture in bottom and up sides of a 10" pie plate.

2 Bake at 375° for 10 to 12 minutes or until lightly browned. Cool completely on a wire rack. Spoon ice cream into prepared crust, and freeze until firm.

3 Beat whipping cream at medium speed of an electric beater until foamy; gradually add powdered sugar, beating until soft peaks form. Spread whipped cream over ice cream layer; top with chocolate curls, if desired.

4 To serve, cut pie into wedges, and drizzle each serving with 1 tablespoon Kahlúa, if desired.

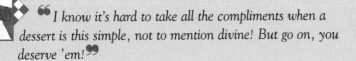

❝ I know it's hard to take all the compliments when a dessert is this simple, not to mention divine! But go on, you deserve 'em! ❞

Black-Bottom Banana Cream Pie

1 (9") pie

1½ cups chocolate graham cracker
     crumbs (about 10 crackers)
⅓ cup butter, melted

1 (3.4-ounce) package vanilla or
     banana cream-flavored instant
     pudding mix
1¼ cups milk
1¾ cups frozen whipped topping,
     thawed and divided

1¼ cups peeled, sliced bananas

1 Preheat the oven to 350°. Combine cracker crumbs and butter, stirring well. Press in bottom and up sides of a 9" pie plate.

2 Bake at 350° for 8 minutes. Remove from oven; let cool on a wire rack.

3 Combine pudding mix and milk in a medium bowl, stirring 1½ minutes with a wire whisk. Gently fold 1 cup whipped topping into pudding mixture. Store remaining whipped topping in refrigerator.

4 Arrange banana slices over prepared crust. Spoon pudding mixture over banana slices. Cover and chill 1½ hours or until set. Pipe or spoon remaining ¾ cup whipped topping around edge of pie just before serving.

Praline-Apple Pie

8 servings

1   (3-pound, 1-ounce) frozen
      deep-dish apple pie

¼   cup butter
1   cup packed brown sugar
⅓   cup whipping cream
1   teaspoon vanilla extract
1   cup powdered sugar
¾   cup chopped pecans, toasted

1 Preheat the oven to 375°. Remove plastic wrap from pie. Open center hole; cut 4 to 6 slits in top crust. Place pie on an aluminum foil-lined baking sheet.

2 Bake at 375° for 1 hour and 20 minutes to 1 hour and 30 minutes, shielding with aluminum foil after 1 hour. Cool 1 hour.

3 Bring butter, brown sugar, and whipping cream to a boil in a 2-quart saucepan over medium heat, stirring often. Boil 1 minute; remove from heat. Whisk in vanilla and powdered sugar until smooth. Pour praline mixture slowly over pie, spreading to cover. Top with pecans.

This Topping's as Easy as Pie

Here, a homemade pecan-and-brown sugar topping spruces up a store-bought apple pie. Dessert has never been so easy—or delicious! You can dress up this apple pie, which comes in a foil pan, simply by placing it in a decorative pie plate!

Easy-as-Pumpkin Pie

1 (9") pie

2   large eggs, lightly beaten
1   (16-ounce) can pumpkin
1   (14-ounce) can sweetened
      condensed milk
1   teaspoon ground cinnamon
½   teaspoon ground ginger
½   teaspoon ground nutmeg
¼   teaspoon salt
1   unbaked 9" frozen pastry shell

Sweetened whipped cream (optional)
Ground nutmeg or cinnamon (optional)

1 Preheat the oven to 350°. Combine first 7 ingredients, and stir well. Pour filling into pastry shell.

2 Bake at 350° for 50 to 55 minutes or until filling is set, shielding edges of piecrust with aluminum foil, if necessary, to prevent overbrowning. Cool on a wire rack. Dollop with sweetened whipped cream, and sprinkle with nutmeg or cinnamon, if desired.

I call this pumpkin pie a dump-and-pour pie 'cause all you've got to do is dump your ingredients into a bowl, mix 'em up, and pour 'em into a pie shell. It's that quick! If you want to jazz it up with sweetened whipped cream, here's how: Whip ½ pint cream with 2 tablespoons powdered sugar and ½ teaspoon vanilla extract in a small bowl with an electric beater.

Peach of a Crisp

6 to 8 servings

1   (29-ounce) can sliced peaches, drained
1   teaspoon grated lemon rind

1   (11-ounce) package piecrust mix
1   cup packed light brown sugar
¼   cup cold butter, cut into small pieces

Vanilla ice cream or frozen yogurt

1 Preheat the oven to 375°. Place peaches in a lightly greased 7" x 11" baking dish. Sprinkle with lemon rind, and set aside.

2 Combine piecrust mix and brown sugar; sprinkle over peaches. Dot with butter.

3 Bake at 375° for 30 minutes. Serve with vanilla ice cream or frozen yogurt.

A Peach of a Dish!
This dish is very versatile, and there's no need to peel fresh peaches! It works well with any kind of canned peaches, from those in heavy syrup to peaches in their own juice. Just choose the type you'd like to use. But keep the can size close to what the recipe calls for so that you'll have the right amount of crust for the fruit. Yum!!

Baked Fruit Turnovers

(pictured on page 174)
6 turnovers

1 (15-ounce) package refrigerated piecrusts
1 cup canned cherry, apple, or peach fruit filling
¼ cup chopped pecans, toasted

1 tablespoon sugar
¼ teaspoon ground cinnamon
Vanilla ice cream (optional)

1 Preheat the oven to 425°. Cut each piecrust into 6 wedges. Combine fruit filling and pecans; spoon evenly in center of 6 wedges. Top with remaining wedges.

2 Moisten edges of pastry with water, pressing edges together. Crimp edges with a fork to seal. Place turnovers on a lightly greased baking sheet. Bake at 425° for 12 to 14 minutes.

3 Combine sugar and cinnamon; sprinkle evenly over warm turnovers. Serve with vanilla ice cream, if desired.

Fast Fry

Fried Fruit Turnovers: Pour vegetable oil into a heavy Dutch oven to depth of 1". Instead of baking as directed in Step 2, fry turnovers, in batches, in hot oil over medium-high heat about 3 to 4 minutes or until golden, turning once. Drain on paper towels. Proceed with Step 3.

Frozen Raspberry Cream

6 servings

1   (14-ounce) package frozen
    raspberries

1   (12-ounce) can frozen pink
    lemonade concentrate

1   quart vanilla ice cream, softened

1 Process frozen raspberries in an electric blender until slushy, stopping once to scrape down sides.

2 Add frozen lemonade concentrate, and process until blended.

3 Add ice cream, and process until smooth, stopping to scrape down sides as needed. Spoon mixture into a 9" x 13" pan. Cover and freeze at least 3 hours. Let stand 5 minutes before serving. To serve, use an ice cream scoop.

"Who would believe that three simple ingredients and three simple steps could create such a sensational summertime treat? Shhh . . . no one has to know how easy it is!!"

Speedy Sorbet

(pictured on facing page)
6 servings

2   (21-ounce) cans blueberry or cherry
       pie filling

1 Freeze unopened cans of pie filling until frozen solid, at least 18 hours or up to 1 month.

2 Submerge unopened can in hot water 1 to 2 minutes. Open both ends of cans, and slide frozen mixture into a bowl. Break into chunks.

3 Process chunks in a food processor until smooth, stopping to scrape down sides as needed.

4 Pour fruit mixture into an 8" square pan. Freeze until firm. Let stand 10 minutes before serving.

One-Ingredient Wonders!

Speedy Pineapple Sorbet: Substitute 2 (20-ounce) cans pineapple chunks in heavy syrup for pie filling. Proceed with Step 1.

Speedy Strawberry Sorbet: Substitute 3 (10-ounce) packages frozen strawberries in syrup for pie filling. Break into chunks, and proceed with Step 3.

Baked Fruit Turnover, page 170

Raspberry Windows, page 191

Triple-Chocolate Bombe

(pictured on facing page)

12 servings

1 (21-ounce) package fudge brownie mix

½ gallon fudge ripple ice cream, softened

½ (16-ounce) can ready-to-spread chocolate fudge frosting

1 (12-ounce) jar raspberry jam, melted (optional)

66 Chocolate lovers, beware! One bite of my chocolaty bombe and you'll be addicted to this fast, fabulous finale! 99

1 Prepare and bake brownies according to package directions, using a 9" x 13" pan. Cool on a wire rack.

2 Cut brownies into squares; press into a 2½-quart freezer-proof bowl lined with plastic wrap, forming a brownie bowl.

3 Spoon softened ice cream into prepared brownie bowl; cover and freeze 8 hours or until firm.

4 Spoon frosting into a microwave-safe bowl. Microwave, covered, at HIGH setting 45 seconds or until melted, stirring well. Invert ice cream bombe onto a platter; coat with melted frosting. To serve, cut into 12 wedges. If desired, spoon 2 tablespoons melted jam onto each serving plate, and top with a bombe wedge. Serve immediately.

Mint-Chocolate Chip Ice Cream Squares

15 servings

3   cups cream-filled chocolate
       sandwich cookie crumbs (about
       30 cookies)
¼   cup butter, melted

½   gallon mint-chocolate chip
       ice cream, slightly softened

1   (11.75-ounce) jar chocolate sauce
1   (12-ounce) container frozen
       whipped topping, thawed
1   cup chopped nuts, toasted

1 Combine cookie crumbs and melted butter. Press into a lightly greased 9" x 13" dish; freeze until firm.

2 Spread ice cream evenly over crust; freeze until firm.

3 Spread chocolate sauce over ice cream; top with whipped topping, and sprinkle with nuts. Freeze until firm.

4 Let stand 10 minutes before serving; cut into squares.

" Just six ingredients make up this frozen dessert. My favorite part? No cooking! Just layer the ingredients, and freeze! "

Decadent Chocolate Pudding

8 servings

2   cups half-and-half
2   egg yolks, lightly beaten
2   tablespoons sugar

3⅓ cups (20 ounces) semisweet
      chocolate chips
3   tablespoons amaretto
2   teaspoons vanilla extract
Pinch of salt

1   cup sweetened whipped cream
Garnish: chocolate shavings

1 Combine first 3 ingredients in a heavy saucepan; cook over medium heat, stirring constantly, 12 minutes or until mixture reaches 160°.

2 Add chocolate chips and next 3 ingredients, stirring until smooth.

3 Spoon into 8 (4-ounce) ramekins or custard cups; cover and chill at least 4 hours. Top each serving with whipped cream. Garnish, if desired.

A Chocolaty Treat!

This dense, rich pudding is a chocolate lover's delight. To make it "family friendly," omit the amaretto and substitute 3 tablespoons milk and ½ teaspoon almond flavoring.

New-Fashioned Banana Pudding

(pictured on back cover)

8 to 10 servings

1	cup milk
2	cups half-and-half
1	(5.1-ounce) package vanilla instant pudding mix

1	(12-ounce) package vanilla wafers
6	large ripe bananas

4	large egg whites
⅓	cup sugar
½	teaspoon vanilla or banana extract

1 Combine milk and half-and-half in a large bowl; add pudding mix, and beat at low speed of an electric beater until blended. Beat at medium speed 2 minutes or until smooth. Set aside.

2 Preheat the oven to 325°. Arrange one-third of vanilla wafers in bottom of a 3-quart baking dish. Slice 2 bananas; layer slices over wafers. Pour one-third of pudding mixture over bananas. Repeat layers twice, arranging wafers around edge of dish.

3 Beat egg whites at high speed of an electric beater until foamy. Add ⅓ cup sugar, 1 tablespoon at a time, beating until stiff peaks form and sugar dissolves (2 to 4 minutes). Fold in vanilla; spread meringue over pudding, sealing to edge of dish.

4 Bake at 325° for 25 minutes or until golden.

Old-Fashioned Appeal

Homemade Vanilla Pudding: If you don't have a box of vanilla pudding on hand, it's easy to make some pudding from scratch! Combine ⅔ cup sugar, ¼ cup all-purpose flour, and a dash of salt in a heavy saucepan. Combine 1 (14-ounce) can sweetened condensed milk with 2½ cups milk and 4 large egg yolks, and whisk into the dry ingredients. Cook over medium heat, whisking constantly, until smooth and thickened. Remove from heat. Stir in 2 teaspoons vanilla. Proceed with Step 2.

Sweet Roll Pudding

4 to 6 servings

2 or 3 large cinnamon-raisin rolls

2 large eggs, lightly beaten
1½ cups milk
¾ cup sugar
1 teaspoon vanilla extract
¼ cup butter, melted
2 tablespoons honey

Caramel ice cream topping

1 Preheat the oven to 300°. Tear enough cinnamon rolls into small pieces to measure 3 cups. Sprinkle torn rolls into a lightly greased shallow 1-quart baking dish.

2 Combine eggs and milk; stir in sugar and vanilla, and pour over torn rolls. Combine butter and honey; pour over roll mixture.

3 Bake at 300° for 1 hour or until golden. Drizzle with caramel topping.

No Leftovers? No Problem!

If you don't have leftover cinnamon-raisin rolls, just buy a package of buns or bake a 7.3-ounce can of refrigerated cinnamon-raisin rolls according to package directions. Tear enough rolls into small chunks to equal the 3 cups, and reserve the packaged frosting for another use.

Chocolate Plunge

7 cups

2   cups light corn syrup
1½   cups whipping cream

3   (12-ounce) packages semisweet
     chocolate chips

1 Combine corn syrup and whipping cream in a heavy saucepan; bring mixture to a boil. Remove from heat.

2 Add chocolate chips, stirring until smooth. Spoon chocolate mixture into a fondue pot or chafing dish. Serve with your favorite dunking morsels (see box below).

Dunking Morsels

The great thing about this chocolate fondue is you can make your own version and dunk almost anything into it. This recipe is perfect with any of the following:

- Pound cake cubes
- Angel food cake cubes
- Fruit slices or chunks (like apples, pears, pineapples, or bananas)
- Whole small fruits (like cherries, strawberries, or grapes)
- Shortbread cookies
- Marshmallows

Cookie Jar Jubilee

"*What's more fun than fixin' a batch of one of my easy cookies or yummy candies? Why, eating them, of course!!***"**

Wedding Cookies

3 dozen

¾ cup butter, softened
½ cup sifted powdered sugar
2 tablespoons honey
1 teaspoon vanilla extract

2 cups all-purpose flour
¼ teaspoon salt
½ cup finely chopped walnuts

Additional powdered sugar

1 Preheat the oven to 325°. Beat butter at medium speed of an electric beater until creamy; add ½ cup powdered sugar and the honey, beating well. Stir in vanilla.

2 Combine flour and salt; add to butter mixture, mixing until well blended. Stir in walnuts.

3 Divide dough into 3 equal portions. Work with 1 portion of dough at a time, storing remainder in refrigerator.

4 Divide each portion of dough into 12 equal pieces. Shape dough into 1" balls, and place 2" apart on lightly greased cookie sheets. Bake at 325° for 14 minutes. Cool slightly on cookie sheets. Roll warm cookies in additional powdered sugar, and cool on wire racks.

Double Up

These dainty little cookies have big flavor! They're packed with nuts and honey and rolled in powdered sugar. "Double dip" them in the powdered sugar if you want them really well coated.

Chunky Hazelnut-Toffee Cookies

4½ dozen

1 cup butter, softened
¾ cup packed brown sugar
½ cup sugar
2 large eggs
1 tablespoon vanilla extract

2¾ cups all-purpose flour
1½ teaspoons baking powder
½ teaspoon baking soda
¼ teaspoon salt

4 (1.4-ounce) English toffee-flavored candy bars, chopped
2 (10-ounce) packages semisweet chocolate chunks
1 cup toasted, chopped hazelnuts or pecans

1 Preheat the oven to 350°. Beat butter at medium speed of an electric beater until creamy. Gradually add sugars, beating well. Add eggs and vanilla, beating mixture well.

2 Combine flour and next 3 ingredients, stirring well. Add to butter mixture, beating at low speed just until blended.

3 Stir in candy bars, chocolate chunks, and nuts. Drop dough by heaping tablespoonfuls 1½" apart onto ungreased cookie sheets.

4 Bake at 350° for 10 minutes or until lightly browned. Let cool slightly on cookie sheets; remove to wire racks to cool completely.

It's hard to resist these cookies chock-full of chocolate and nuts. Wanna know my secret to taking the skins off hazelnuts? Just cook 'em with 1 teaspoon baking soda in boiling water 30 to 45 seconds. Drain the nuts; rub them with a dish towel, and the skins will come right off. Make sure you dry them completely before toasting.

Rum-Raisin Macaroons

4 dozen

2   (7-ounce) packages flaked coconut
     (5⅓ cups total)
1   (14-ounce) can sweetened
     condensed milk
1   cup chopped macadamia nuts,
     toasted
1   cup chocolate-covered raisins
2   teaspoons vanilla extract
½   teaspoon rum extract

1 Preheat the oven to 350°. Combine all ingredients in a large bowl; stir well. Drop dough by level tablespoonfuls onto greased cookie sheets.

2 Bake at 350° for 10 minutes or until edges are lightly browned. Let stand 1 minute on cookie sheets; remove to wire racks to cool completely.

❝Go ahead and splurge on the macadamia nuts for the perfect accent to these coconut drop cookies. And if you have some of the nuts left over, store them in the refrigerator or freezer to prevent them from becoming rancid.❞

Easy Ginger Cookies

3 dozen

1   (14-ounce) package gingerbread
    mix
⅔   cup water
½   cup chunky or creamy peanut butter

½   cup raisins

1 Preheat the oven to 350°. Combine first 3 ingredients in a large bowl, stirring until smooth.

2 Add raisins; stir well. Drop dough by rounded teaspoonfuls onto greased cookie sheets.

3 Bake at 350° for 10 to 12 minutes. Cool 5 minutes on cookie sheets; remove to wire racks to cool completely.

Peanut Butter and Jelly Cookies

2 dozen

⅓ cup butter, softened
¼ cup creamy peanut butter
¾ cup packed brown sugar
1 large egg
1 teaspoon vanilla extract

1¾ cups all-purpose flour
½ teaspoon baking soda

⅔ cup strawberry jam or grape jelly

1 Preheat the oven to 350°. Beat butter and peanut butter at medium speed with an electric beater until creamy. Gradually add brown sugar, beating well. Add egg and vanilla, beating well.

2 Combine flour and baking soda; gradually add to butter mixture, mixing well.

3 Shape dough into 1" balls, and place 2" apart on ungreased cookie sheets. Flatten balls in a crisscross pattern with a floured fork. Bake at 350° for 9 minutes or until lightly browned. Cool 1 minute on cookie sheets; remove to wire racks to cool completely.

4 Spread jam on bottoms of half the cookies; top with remaining cookies.

A Classic Combination!
The dynamic duo of peanut butter and jelly does it again in this sandwich cookie that kids of all ages will love! To make them even faster, use peanut butter slice-and-bake cookie dough instead of my homemade dough.

Molasses Crinkles

4 dozen

¾ cup shortening
1 cup packed brown sugar
1 large egg
¼ cup molasses

2¼ cups all-purpose flour
2 teaspoons baking soda
1 teaspoon ground cinnamon
1 teaspoon ground ginger
½ teaspoon ground cloves
¼ teaspoon salt

Sugar

1 Preheat the oven to 350°. Beat shortening at medium speed with an electric beater until creamy; gradually add brown sugar, beating well. Add egg and molasses, beating well.

2 Combine flour and next 5 ingredients; add to shortening mixture, mixing well.

3 Shape dough into 1" balls, and roll each ball in sugar. Place 2" apart on lightly greased cookie sheets.

4 Bake at 350° for 10 to 14 minutes. Cool on cookie sheets 3 minutes. Remove to wire racks to cool completely.

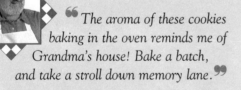

❝ The aroma of these cookies baking in the oven reminds me of Grandma's house! Bake a batch, and take a stroll down memory lane. ❞

Cherry Ice Box Cookies

4 dozen

1   cup butter, softened
1   cup granulated sugar
1   large egg
1   teaspoon vanilla extract

2¾   cups all-purpose flour
1   teaspoon baking powder
½   teaspoon salt
1   (16-ounce) jar maraschino
      cherries, drained and finely
      chopped
1   cup finely chopped nuts

¼   cup red decorator sugar (optional)

1 Beat butter at medium speed of an electric beater until creamy. Gradually add 1 cup granulated sugar, beating well. Add egg and vanilla, beating well.

2 Combine flour, baking powder, and salt; add to butter mixture, beating well. Pat cherries between paper towels to remove excess moisture. Stir cherries and nuts into dough; cover dough, and chill 2 hours.

3 Shape dough into 2 (1½" x 8") logs. Roll in red decorator sugar, if desired. Wrap logs in wax paper, and freeze 2 hours or until firm. (Store in freezer up to 6 months, if desired.)

4 Preheat the oven to 400°. Unwrap frozen dough, and slice into ¼"-thick slices, using a sharp knife. Place on lightly greased cookie sheets. (Do not let thaw.)

5 Bake at 400° for 8 to 10 minutes or until golden. Let cool 1 minute on cookie sheets. Transfer to wire racks to cool completely.

All-Occasion Cookies

These nutty slice 'n' bake cookies are perfect for any occasion. They're great for an after-school snack or drop-in guests.

Raspberry Windows

(pictured on page 175)

2 dozen

2   (18-ounce) rolls refrigerated
       sliceable sugar cookie dough

Powdered sugar

½   cup seedless raspberry or
      currant jelly

1 Freeze cookie dough 30 minutes. Preheat the oven to 350°. Working with 1 roll of dough at a time, cut roll into ¼"-wide slices. Place slices on ungreased cookie sheets.

2 Bake at 350° for 10 minutes or until edges are golden. Remove from oven, and immediately use a 1" cutter or a clean plastic bottle cap to cut out a round in center of half the cookies. Cool cookies on cookie sheets 1 minute; transfer to wire racks to cool completely.

4 Sift powdered sugar over cookie cutouts. Spread each solid cookie with about ½ teaspoon raspberry jelly; top each with a cookie cutout.

" Refrigerated cookie dough is my secret to making cookies that win oohs and aahs from the after-school gang or your friends at a cookie swap! And in addition to these pretty sandwich cookies, you'll have 2 dozen 1" round cookies left over for nibbling. That's my kind of recipe!! "

Butter Meltaways

3 dozen

1   cup butter, softened
⅓   cup sifted powdered sugar
1¼   cups all-purpose flour
¾   cup cornstarch

Lemon Frosting

1 Beat butter at medium speed of an electric beater until creamy; gradually add ⅓ cup powdered sugar, beating well. Combine flour and cornstarch; gradually add to butter mixture, beating just until blended. Chill dough. Shape into 2 (6") logs; wrap in wax paper dusted with powdered sugar. Chill at least 4 hours.

2 Preheat the oven to 350°. Unwrap dough. Cut each log into 18 slices; place slices 2" apart on greased cookie sheets. Bake at 350° for 8 minutes. Transfer to wire racks to cool completely. Spread cookies with Lemon Frosting.

Lemon Frosting

3   cups sifted powdered sugar
2½   tablespoons lemon juice
2   tablespoons milk
1   drop of red or yellow liquid food
        color (optional)

Combine all ingredients, stirring well. Yield: ¾ cup.

Careful Coloring
One drop of food color goes a long way! To get the right amount, drop food color on a plate, and transfer it to the frosting with a wooden toothpick. This way, you'll be able to control the color you want.

Peanut Butter Brownie Cups

15 brownie cups

1   (21-ounce) package chewy fudge
    brownie mix
15 miniature peanut butter cup candies

1 Preheat the oven to 350°. Prepare brownie mix according to package directions.

2 Spoon batter into paper-lined muffin pans, filling two-thirds full. Unwrap candies; place 1 candy in center of each muffin cup, pressing down until batter meets top edge of candy. Bake at 350° for 20 minutes. Carefully remove from pan; let cool completely on wire racks.

" Snuggled within each of these chewy fudgy brownies is a tiny peanut butter cup candy. When I'm in the mood for more cake-like brownies, I just bake the brownie cups a minute longer. "

Caramel-Walnut Brownies

15 brownies

1   (14-ounce) package caramels
⅔   cup evaporated milk, divided

1   (18.25-ounce) package
      caramel-flavored cake mix
¾   cup butter, melted
2   teaspoons vanilla extract
¾   teaspoon ground cinnamon

1½ cups walnut halves or pieces

1 Preheat the oven to 350°. Unwrap caramels, and place in a medium saucepan. Add ⅓ cup evaporated milk; cook over low heat until caramels melt, stirring often. Remove from heat.

2 Combine remaining ⅓ cup milk, the dry cake mix, and next 3 ingredients; stir just until blended. Spread half of dough into a lightly greased 9" square pan. Chill remaining dough. Bake at 350° for 10 minutes. Cool in pan on a wire rack 5 minutes.

3 Pour warm caramel mixture over brownie layer in pan. Sprinkle with walnuts. Spoon remaining half of dough into 9 equal portions on wax paper. Pat each portion into a 3" circle. Place circles over walnuts in pan, overlapping slightly. (Dough will spread during baking.)

4 Bake at 350° for 25 minutes. Cool completely in pan on a wire rack. Cover; chill thoroughly before cutting into squares.

A Devilish Delight

Chocolate-Caramel-Walnut Brownies: Substitute devil's food cake mix for caramel-flavored cake mix. Omit the cinnamon, and bake 30 minutes instead of the 25 minutes in Step 4.

Gooey Turtle Bars

2 dozen

1   cup butter, melted
1   (12-ounce) box vanilla wafer
    cookies, finely crushed
1   (12-ounce) package semisweet
    chocolate chips
1   (12-ounce) jar caramel topping
    or 1 (12.25-ounce) jar fat-free
    caramel topping
1   cup coarsely chopped pecans

1 Preheat the oven to 350°. Combine butter and wafer crumbs in a 9" x 13" baking pan; press into pan. Sprinkle with chocolate chips; drizzle with caramel topping, and sprinkle with pecans.

2 Bake at 350° for 18 to 20 minutes or until chips melt; cool completely in pan on a wire rack. Chill at least 2 hours; cut into bars.

" 'Gooey' is right! Chocolate, caramel, and pecans make up the decadent topping that covers a rich, buttery crust. And just one bite of these sensational bars will have you saying 'OOH IT'S SO GOOD!!'"

Lemon Glacier Bars

15 bars

1   (18.25-ounce) package lemon
      cake mix
1   large egg
1/3 cup vegetable oil

1   (8-ounce) package cream cheese,
      softened
1/3 cup sugar
1   large egg
2   teaspoons lemon juice

1 Preheat the oven to 350°. Combine cake mix, 1 egg, and oil in a large mixing bowl; beat at medium speed of an electric beater until crumbly. Reserve 1 cup cake mixture for topping. Press remaining cake mixture into an ungreased 9" x 13" pan.

2 Bake at 350° for 12 minutes or until lightly browned.

3 Beat cream cheese at medium speed until creamy; add sugar, 1 egg, and lemon juice, beating until smooth. Pour cream cheese mixture over baked crust; sprinkle with reserved 1 cup cake mixture.

4 Bake, uncovered, at 350° for 20 to 22 minutes or until lightly browned. Let cool slightly; cover and chill. Cut into bars.

Cocoa-Almond Biscotti

2 dozen

½ cup butter, softened
1 cup sugar
2 large eggs
1½ tablespoons Kahlúa or cooled strong
    coffee

2½ cups all-purpose flour
1½ teaspoons baking powder
¼ teaspoon salt
3 tablespoons cocoa
1 (6-ounce) can whole almonds

" Biscotti are long-slivered, intensely crunchy Italian cookies. I think they're perfect for dunking into a cup of hot coffee!"

1 Preheat the oven to 350°. Beat butter and sugar in a large bowl at medium speed of an electric beater until light and fluffy. Add eggs, beating well. Stir in Kahlúa or coffee.

2 Combine flour and next 3 ingredients; add to butter mixture, beating at low speed until blended. Stir in almonds. Divide dough in half; using floured hands, shape each portion into a 2" x 9" log on a lightly greased cookie sheet.

3 Bake at 350° for 28 to 30 minutes or until firm. Cool on cookie sheet 5 minutes. Remove to a wire rack to cool.

4 Cut each log diagonally into ¾"-thick slices with a serrated knife, using a gentle sawing motion. Place on ungreased cookie sheets. Bake 5 minutes. Turn cookies over; bake 5 to 6 more minutes. Remove to wire racks to cool.

Party Berries in Chocolate

2 dozen

1   (6-ounce) package premium white chocolate squares

6   (1-ounce) semisweet chocolate squares, coarsely chopped

24 large fresh strawberries (about 2 pints), rinsed and dried thoroughly with paper towels

1 Place white chocolate in a microwave-safe bowl. Microwave 1 to 2 minutes at MEDIUM setting (50% power). Remove from microwave, and stir constantly until completely melted. Microwave semisweet chocolate 1 to 2 minutes at MEDIUM setting (50% power). Remove from microwave; stir until completely melted.

2 Hold berries by stems; dip half of berries into melted white chocolate, turning to coat. Place on lightly greased, wax paper-lined baking sheets. Dip remaining berries in melted semisweet chocolate. Chill until firm. Serve within 8 hours.

Note: I used a 700-watt microwave.

Best-Dressed Berries

Here's how to dress up Party Berries in a tux! Melt white chocolate according to Step 1. Dip strawberries into melted white chocolate; place on wax paper-lined baking sheets. Chill until firm. Melt semisweet chocolate according to Step 1. Dip each side of coated strawberry halfway into chocolate, forming a "V." Chill until firm. Spoon remaining semisweet chocolate into a zip-top plastic bag; seal. Prick a tiny hole in one corner of bag with a toothpick; pipe a bow tie and 3 buttons onto strawberries to resemble tuxedos. Chill until firm.

Butterscotch-Peanut Fudge

2½ pounds

1 (11-ounce) package butterscotch chips
1 (14-ounce) can sweetened condensed milk
1½ cups miniature marshmallows

⅔ cup chunky peanut butter
1 teaspoon vanilla extract
⅛ teaspoon salt
1 cup chopped dry-roasted peanuts

1 Cook first 3 ingredients in a small heavy saucepan over medium heat, stirring constantly, 5 to 6 minutes or until smooth; remove from heat.

2 Stir in peanut butter, vanilla, and salt until blended; stir in peanuts. Pour into a buttered 9-inch square pan. Chill until firm; cut into squares. Store in refrigerator.

Note: If desired, microwave first 3 ingredients in a 2-quart microwave-safe bowl at HIGH setting 2 to 3 minutes or until melted, stirring twice.

Caramelts

16 squares

1   (14-ounce) package caramels
¼   cup milk

4   cups crisp rice cereal
1   cup salted roasted peanuts

1 Unwrap caramels, and place in a large saucepan. Add milk; cook over low heat until caramels melt, stirring often. Remove from heat.

2 Stir in cereal and peanuts. Spoon into a buttered 8" square pan. Firmly press mixture into pan. Cool completely in pan on a wire rack. Cut into squares.

I love how simple these sweet caramel treats are to make! The crisp rice cereal and peanuts add a fun crunch that will delight kids of all ages!!

White Chocolate Candy

40 candies

8   (2-ounce) vanilla-flavored almond bark candy coating squares, coarsely chopped

3   cups pretzel sticks, broken into 1-inch pieces

1   cup Spanish peanuts

1 Place candy coating in a microwave-safe bowl. Microwave at HIGH setting 1 to 2 minutes or until coating melts, stirring twice.

2 Add pretzels and peanuts, stirring to coat. Drop by tablespoonfuls onto wax paper-lined baking sheets. Chill until firm.

Chocolaty Treats

These two-step pretzel-peanut candies are a sweet and salty delight! You can change them up some by using chocolate-flavored candy instead of the vanilla-flavored candy coating. Either way, these candies are real crowd-pleasers!!

Peanut Clusters

4 dozen

8 (2-ounce) vanilla-flavored almond bark candy coating squares, coarsely chopped
2⅔ cups milk chocolate chips
1 pound salted Spanish peanuts

1 Melt candy coating and chocolate chips in a heavy saucepan over low heat, stirring constantly. Remove from heat; stir in peanuts.

2 Drop mixture by tablespoonfuls onto wax paper-lined baking sheets. Chill until firm.

You'll have sweet dreams with this quick confection! My recipe uses only three ingredients, and it's practically foolproof! For ease, microwave the candy coating and chocolate chips in a 1-quart microwave-safe bowl at HIGH setting 2 to 3 minutes or until chocolate melts, stirring twice.

Microwave Pecan Brittle

¾ pound

1 cup sugar
½ cup light corn syrup

1 cup pecan or nut pieces
1 teaspoon butter
1 teaspoon vanilla extract
1 teaspoon baking soda

1 Combine sugar and corn syrup in a microwave-safe bowl, stirring well. Cover with heavy-duty plastic wrap, and microwave at HIGH setting 4 minutes.

2 Add pecans, stirring well. Microwave at HIGH setting 4 minutes or until lightly browned. Stir in butter and vanilla; microwave at HIGH setting 1 minute. Stir in baking soda until foamy.

3 Immediately pour mixture onto a lightly greased baking sheet; let cool on baking sheet on a wire rack. Break into pieces; store in an airtight container.

Note: For testing this recipe, I used a 700-watt microwave.

Go Nuts!
This brittle recipe works well with your favorite nut—try peanuts, cashews, walnuts, or even exotic macadamias for your own special recipe!

METRIC EQUIVALENTS

The recipes that appear in this cookbook use the standard United States method for measuring liquid and dry or solid ingredients (teaspoons, tablespoons, and cups). The information in the following charts is provided to help cooks outside the U.S. successfully use these recipes. All equivalents are approximate.

EQUIVALENTS FOR DIFFERENT TYPES OF INGREDIENTS

A standard cup measure of a dry or solid ingredient will vary in weight depending on the type of ingredient. A standard cup of liquid is the same volume for any type of liquid. Use the following chart when converting standard cup measures to grams (weight) or milliliters (volume).

Standard Cup	Fine Powder	Grain	Granular	Liquid Solids	Liquid
	(ex. flour)	(ex. rice)	(ex. sugar)	(ex. butter)	(ex. milk)
1	140 g	150 g	190 g	200 g	240 ml
¾	105 g	113 g	143 g	150 g	180 ml
⅔	93 g	100 g	125 g	133 g	160 ml
½	70 g	75 g	95 g	100 g	120 ml
⅓	47 g	50 g	63 g	67 g	80 ml
¼	35 g	38 g	48 g	50 g	60 ml
⅛	18 g	19 g	24 g	25 g	30 ml

DRY INGREDIENTS BY WEIGHT

(To convert ounces to grams, multiply the number of ounces by 30.)

1 oz	=	¹⁄₁₆ lb	=	30 g
4 oz	=	¼ lb	=	120 g
8 oz	=	½ lb	=	240 g
12 oz	=	¾ lb	=	360 g
16 oz	=	1 lb	=	480 g

LENGTH

(To convert inches to centimeters, multiply the number of inches by 2.5.)

1 in				=	2.5 cm		
6 in	=	½ ft		=	15 cm		
12 in	=	1 ft		=	30 cm		
36 in	=	3 ft	=	1 yd	=	90 cm	
40 in				=	100 cm	=	1 meter

LIQUID INGREDIENTS BY VOLUME

¼ tsp						=	1 ml	
½ tsp						=	2 ml	
1 tsp						=	5 ml	
3 tsp	=	1 tbls			=	½ fl oz	=	15 ml
		2 tbls	=	⅛ cup	=	1 fl oz	=	30 ml
		4 tbls	=	¼ cup	=	2 fl oz	=	60 ml
		5⅓ tbls	=	⅓ cup	=	3 fl oz	=	80 ml
		8 tbls	=	½ cup	=	4 fl oz	=	120 ml
		10⅔ tbls	=	⅔ cup	=	5 fl oz	=	160 ml
		12 tbls	=	¾ cup	=	6 fl oz	=	180 ml
		16 tbls	=	1 cup	=	8 fl oz	=	240 ml
		1 pt	=	2 cups	=	16 fl oz	=	480 ml
		1 qt	=	4 cups	=	32 fl oz	=	960 ml
						33 fl oz	=	1000 ml = 1 liter

COOKING/OVEN TEMPERATURES

	Fahrenheit	Celsius	Gas Mark
Freeze Water	32° F	0° C	
Room Temperature	68° F	20° C	
Boil Water	212° F	100° C	
Bake	325° F	160° C	3
	350° F	180° C	4
	375° F	190° C	5
	400° F	200° C	6
	425° F	220° C	7
	450° F	230° C	8
Broil			Grill

Index